A SEASON OF TRIUMPH

The Official Commemorative of the 2001 Baseball Season

A SEASON OF TRIUMPH

Table of Contents

Division Series

Championship Series

Acknowledgements

To watch this year's World Series was to watch two extraordinary teams. Sure, the Yankees and Diamondbacks had players who may have shined more than others, but those clubs will tell you their success was a team effort.

The success of this book project was a team effort as well. If not for each and every contribution made to this book, it couldn't have been done as well and as quickly as it was.

Don Hintze and Mike McCormick at Major League Baseball gave us the support to do this book and helped fine-tune the content. Rich Pilling, Paul Cunningham and MLB's cadre of photographers tracked down and provided some of the lasting images you will see in this book. Some of those images will never be forgotten.

At *The Sporting News*, Pete Newcomb edited countless rolls of film, shot by a group of talented photographers—Albert Dickson, Bob Leverone, Robert Seale and Dilip Vishwanat, whose work was coordinated by Fred Barnes. They were our eyes for the entire season.

No one loves the game of baseball more than TSN Senior Editor Joe Hoppel; it was an easy decision to turn this project over to him because we all know his passion for the game will be expressed in quality work. Ron Smith, as always, lent his guidance and editing, along with Jeff Paur and David Walton, who dropped other responsibilities and took on this one.

Art direction was provided by Bob Parajon, with a huge assist from Bill Wilson. Designers Michael Behrens, Matt Kindt, Jack Kruyne, Chad Painter and Christen Sager also lent their talents to produce this book. Bob, too, directed the staff of Chris Barnes-Amaro, Dave Brickey and Steve Romer and oversaw the flow of hundreds of images, ensuring the quality was, well, of exceptional quality. Finally, Russ Carr gave the pages a final look and put on the finishing touches before sending them off to our printer.

Good things happen with team efforts. We think you'll find one right here.

Produced in partnership and licensed by Major League Baseball Properties, Inc.

Executive Vice President	Timothy J. Brosnan
Vice President of Publishing	Donald S. Hintze
Editor	Michael J. McCormick
Manager, MLB Photos	Rich Pilling
Photo Editor	Paul Cunningham

Published by The Sporting News, 10176 Corporate Square Drive, Suite 200, St. Louis, MO 63132.

ISBN: 0-89204-683-X

Photo Credits

T = top, C = center, B = bottom, L = left, R = right.

Major League Baseball Photos:
Rich Pilling: 2, 8B, 10R, 12, 14, 15T, 15B, 18, 20, 36L, 40T, 40C, 40B, 41, 60L, 60R, 65TR, 80L, 82, 84R, 86, 89, 102T, 102B, 103T, 128L, 130TL, 130TR, 130BC, 137.
Denis Brodeur: 11T.
Bill Stover: 11B, 37.
Robert Beck: 16B.
Allen Kee: 22T, 27, 34R.
Ben Van Houten: 42, 52, 79.
Mark Levine: 51BR.
Brad Mangin: 101BR, 106TL, 106TR, 106CL, 107L, 122B, 123TL, 123B, 128R, 138BL, 139BC, 139BR, 142TR, 142C, 142B, 143TR, 143CR, 143BR.
Ron Vesely: 103BC, 113TR, 118B, 142TL.

The Sporting News:
Albert Dickson: 9T, 24C, 24BL, 24BC, 25, 28B, 28R, 33BR, 43T, 44, 46T, 46B, 47T, 47B, 49BR, 90T, 90R, 91T, 92B, 93T, 94, 95TL, 95BR, 95C, 96L, 98, 99L, 99R, 100, 101L, 101TR, 129BR, 130TC, 130CL, 130CC, 130CR, 130BL, 130BR, 131L, 131R, 132, 134TL, 134TR, 134B, 135TL, 136, 138R, 139TR, 141T, 141BL.
Dilip Vishwanat: 9B, 32, 33T, 48, 76, 77, 78T, 78B.
Robert Seale: 10L, 49T, 49BL, 70T, 71, 72L, 73BR, 75, 88, 90CL, 91B, 92T, 93B, 95TR, 96R, 103BR, 105, 106CR, 107R, 109L, 109R, 110BL, 110BR, 112L, 113L, 113BR, 114TR, 114B, 115R, 116B, 118TL, 119, 122TR, 123TR, 126BL, 126R, 127, 129TR, 135R, 138TL, 140T, 140B, 141BR, 143L.
John Dunn for The Sporting News: 35L, 80R, 81T, 81R, 103BL, 104, 106B, 108, 110TL, 110TR, 111TR, 111B, 114TL, 115L, 116T, 118TR, 121, 122TL, 124TL, 124R, 124BL, 125T, 125BL, 125BR, 126TL.
Bob Leverone: 4, 17, 31.
Rod Mar for The Sporting News: 24T.
John Cordes for The Sporting News: 43B.

The Baltimore Sun:
Gene Sweeney Jr.: 23B.
Elizabeth Malby: 26, 28T.

AP/Wide World Photos:
16T, 22C, 22B, 23T, 30T, 30B, 33BL, 34TL, 35R, 38TL, 38R, 38BL, 39T, 39C, 39BL, 39BR, 50T, 50BL, 50BR, 51T, 51BL, 54, 55T, 55B, 56, 57T, 57B, 58T, 58B, 59, 61CR, 61T, 61B, 62, 63, 64L, 64R, 65BR, 66R, 66BL, 67R, 68, 69T, 69B, 70B, 72R, 73T, 74, 83, 84L.

Front Cover:
American Flag (John Dunn for The Sporting News); Diamondbacks celebration (Rich Pilling/MLB Photos); Ichiro Suzuki (Albert Dickson/The Sporting News) Tony Gwynn (AP/Wide World Photos); Cal Ripken Jr. (Mark Levine/MLB Photos); Barry Bonds (Bob Leverone/The Sporting News).

Back Cover:
Sammy Sosa (AP/Wide World Photos).

INTRODUCTION

A triumphant spirit wins out

It was a season of records and milestones, a season of superstar careers at their end and superstar careers just emerging. It was a season of crowning moments and achievements. It was a season of triumph.

Ultimately, it was a season of triumph for the Arizona Diamondbacks. But when Luis Gonzalez put an exclamation mark on a seven-game World Series with a game-winning, ninth-inning single, it not only capped a captivating Fall Classic, it capped a classic season.

New ballparks were christened in Pittsburgh and Milwaukee, and St. Louis rookie Albert Pujols left his mark on the National League. Rickey Henderson didn't just reach 3,000 hits in his illustrious career, he also surpassed Ty Cobb as the leader in career runs scored and Babe Ruth as No. 1 in walks. Ichiro mania swept Seattle, and Japan, as the Mariners tied the record for most wins in a season—116. Tony Gwynn and Cal Ripken played their final games, ending their splendid playing careers. Mike Mussina came agonizingly close to a perfect game. And Barry Bonds extended one of baseball's most treasured single-season marks—home runs in a season—with an almost unthinkable total of 73.

And just when you thought that couldn't be topped, along came the World Series. The never-say-die spirit of the Yankees and Diamondbacks gave us heart-stopping moments in Games 4, 5 and 7. Curt Schilling and Randy Johnson and Roger Clemens pitched splendidly, and there were clutch hits at every turn.

It was a season of triumph.

In the heart of the pennant races, in the heart of Barry Bonds' chase of Mark McGwire's home run record, tragedy struck on September 11. Terrorists attacked New York and Washington, D.C. More victims lay in a field in Pennsylvania, and all Americans—from East to West—became emotional and physical victims of the violence.

Baseball shut down for a week. Shea Stadium, site just one year earlier for half of baseball's Subway Series, became a staging ground for rescue efforts in New York City. Mets and Yankees and players from visiting teams offered their support,

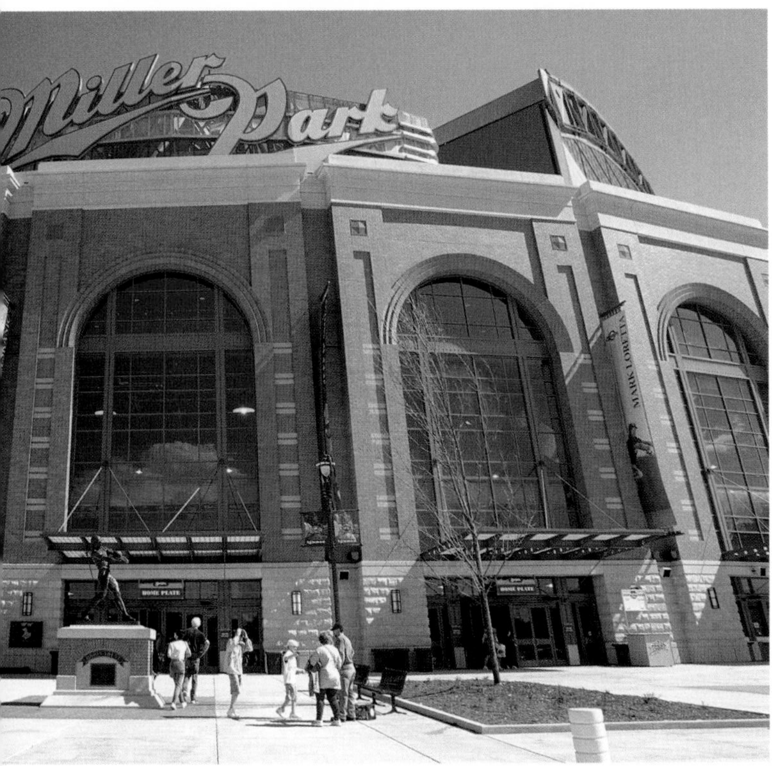

NEW FACES: Newcomers drawing attention in 2001 included Seattle's Ichiro Suzuki (top) and the Cardinals' Albert Pujols. Suzuki, who became known simply as Ichiro, won the American League batting title in his first year in the States. Pujols, only 21, set a National League rookie record for RBIs in a season. Also earning rave reviews in their debuts: Milwaukee's Miller Park and Pittsburgh's PNC Park.

HEADLINERS: **Barry Bonds was applauded time and again for what he accomplished in 2001, and Tony Gwynn and Cal Ripken won ovations for what they had achieved over two sterling decades. Bonds did the unthinkable, breaking Mark McGwire's season home run record; Gwynn and Ripken wound up magnificent careers with stirring farewell tours.**

helping at the staging ground and visiting Ground Zero.

Yankee Stadium, long a sacred venue for not just Yankees fans but all baseball fans, became a site for an emotional prayer service, honoring those men and women who died at the World Trade Center and those courageous people who died in the line of duty.

And when the games resumed, players—heroes to millions of kids throughout the world—responded by deflecting that status to real heroes: firefighters, police officers, rescue workers and emergency-response teams. They wore the flag proudly on their uniforms, they wore "FDNY" and "NYPD" caps to honor the firefighters and police.

And we sang. "The Star-Spangled Banner" was sung loudly and respectfully. "God Bless America" was sung as a prayerful plea. The National Pastime became part of the healing of the national tragedy.

And after President George W. Bush stood on the mound at Yankee Stadium and threw out the ceremonial first pitch for Game 3 of the World Series, doing so just a few miles from the most horrific attack on American soil, he walked off with a thumbs-up salute to the fans, to America, and the crowd chanted "U-S-A! U-S-A! U-S-A!"

There was no greater triumph than that.

NO ONE WILL FORGET: When baseball went back to work after the September 11 terrorist attacks, there were solemn, patriotic and uplifting ceremonies throughout the major leagues. Among the typical scenes were those in Montreal, where Expos and Marlins players paid tribute to the victims of the New York, Washington, D.C., and Pennsylvania tragedies, and St. Louis, where Cardinals players watched an emotional video depicting U.S. values.

2001 Regular Season

BANCO
POPULAR
TRIPLE-S
ESSSE ES MI PLAN
VISIT
PUERTO
RICO!
RadioShack
Si tienes
preguntas,
hack
AY 2001
APRIL 1
UERTO RICO

PLAY BALL! The major league season, which began in Mexico in 1999 and in Japan in 2000, started in Puerto Rico in 2001 when featuring a ceremonial pitch by Hall of Famer and Puerto Rican legend Orlando Cepeda (opposite page, top) and the waving of a Puerto

Toronto played Texas. Raul Mondesi and the Blue Jays won, 8-1, on a day Rican flag by native son Ivan Rodriguez, the Rangers' star catcher.

NOMO'S NO-NO: Making his first start as a member of the Red Sox, Hideo Nomo tossed a no-hitter at Baltimore and got a big hug from batterymate Jason Varitek. Brian Daubach (left) homered and drove in all of Boston's runs in the 3-0 victory. Nomo had pitched a no-hit game in the National League in 1996, accomplishing the feat for the Dodgers.

Albert Pujols, who spent virtually all of the 2000 season in the low minors, was a revelation for a Cardinals team that made a late surge into the playoffs. Pujols, 21, hit .329 (sixth-best in the league) with 37 homers and set an N.L. rookie mark with 130 RBIs.

The Diamondbacks' Luis Gonzalez, who had hit a career-high 31 home runs in 2000, had 32 by the end of June and went on to finish with 57 homers. He established a National League record—and tied the major league mark—with 13 home runs in April.

MILLER TIME: After playing their first 31 seasons in County Stadium, the Milwaukee Brewers moved into Miller Park. The Brewers' first home series, played April 6-7-8, was an artistic and financial success, with Milwaukee sweeping the Cincinnati Reds and drawing a total of more than 116,000 fans to the three games. President George W. Bush was on hand for the opener.

16 17 18 19 20 21 22 23 24 25 26 27 28 29 30

PNC PARK
HOME OF THE PITTSBURGH PIRATES
BUD LIGHT
Jeff
Bagwell
PNC
GIANT EAGLE

THE PRIDE OF PITTSBURGH: With Pittsburgh's skyline and river and bridge views offering a spectacular backdrop, the Pirates' PNC Park made its debut as one of the most scenic venues in baseball. There was a sad note, though: On April 9, the day PNC opened, Willie Stargell, one of the most popular players in Pirates history, died after a long illness.

A WILD NO-HITTER, 20 STRIKEOUTS: Marlins righthander A.J. Burnett, who entered the game with seven career victories in the majors, threw a no-hitter at San Diego and was a 3-0 winner against the Padres despite allowing nine walks. Four days before Burnett was mobbed by his teammates, Arizona's Randy Johnson tied a major league record with 20 strikeouts over nine innings but failed to get the decision in a game in which the Diamondbacks edged Cincinnati, 4-3, in 11 innings. In contrast to Burnett's wild streak, Johnson did not issue a base on balls in his scintillating performance on May 8 at Bank One Ballpark in Phoenix.

After slugging a ninth-inning home run at San Diego on June 16 to complete the second cycle of his major league career, Seattle's John Olerud received congratulations from teammate Mark McLemore. Olerud previously had singled, doubled, tripled and homered in the same game while playing for the Mets in 1997. Strangely, Olerud had only one triple in all of '97 and just one in 2001.

At a June 19 news conference in Baltimore attended by his wife Kelly, Iron Man Cal Ripken announced he would retire at season's end. The disclosure soon set into motion a farewell tour for the popular Ripken, who was playing his 21st season with the Orioles.

Oh, Ichiro!

Oh, the doubters!

Sure, Ichiro Suzuki had won seven consecutive batting titles in Japan, but skeptics wondered if a position player could make the transition to big-league ball in the States. Pitchers had some success while making the Japan-to-U.S. switch, but the prospect of a slightly built everyday player enduring the grind of a long U.S. season and thriving seemed questionable.

So much for the naysayers.

Signed by the Mariners in November 2000, Suzuki reeled off 15- and 23-game hitting streaks in the first 6½ weeks of the 2001 season—and became an instant sensation. He was hitting .349 at the end of June and bound for the All-Star Game (far right).

Soon known by his first name

(befitting a celebrity), Ichiro went on to lead the A.L. in batting (.350), steals (56) and hits (242, a major league record for a rookie).

Ripken made certain that his son, Ryan, had an up-close view of batting practice at the All-Star Game. Later, Ryan sat alongside his father when Dad fielded questions from the media after winning MVP honors in the game, which the A.L. won, 4-1.

Homage paid to Gwynn, Ripken

When Baltimore's Cal Ripken and San Diego's Tony Gwynn announced in June that they would retire at the end of the 2001 season, baseball set out to honor two of the most notable and respected players in the game's history.

Tributes were paid to the two standouts at the All-Star Game in July and then on regular-season farewell tours throughout both leagues, where fans in rival outposts and in the players' home cities showered Ripken and Gwynn with praise, applause and gifts for jobs exceptionally well done. And done with inestimable class.

Ripken and Gwynn shared an uncommon love and devotion for the game, as well as a commitment to play it in a fundamentally sound way. They had their differences, though.

Ripken was the ultimate lunch-bucket type, a man who just wouldn't call in sick. Despite 400-plus homers and more than 3,000 hits, he was not a great natural talent—as countless batting stances and constant tinkering with his game proved. But Ripken was a great natural leader, one who led by example. The best example of all: breaking Lou Gehrig's consecutive-games record in 1995 and pulling the game out of its post-strike funk with that heroic effort.

Gwynn was one of the best pure hitters the game has ever known. His sweet swing accounted for a remarkable eight National League batting crowns and a .338 career batting average. And his sweet disposition accounted for a special bond with fans who like their heroes upbeat, uplifting and accessible.

Worthy of special sendoffs, Ripken and Gwynn received just that as the season wound down.

After acknowledging a standing ovation from the Safeco Field crowd (top) at the All-Star Game, Ripken swung at the first pitch he saw in the game and homered to left field—which sparked another rousing reaction from the fans. Gwynn, an honorary player for the N.L. squad, got a warm reception when he received an award from commissioner Bud Selig.

NGERS
3
ARINERS
new era cap.com
SHAU
01

The BIG rally

Trailing by a 12-0 score in the third inning is one thing. Down 14-2 as late as the seventh inning is another. And falling 12 runs behind a Seattle team boasting an 80-30 record is yet another impossible hurdle.

Make that improbable, not impossible.

The Cleveland Indians, in an amazing turnabout at Jacobs Field, struck for three runs in the seventh inning, four in the eighth and five in the ninth to tie the Mariners, 14-14. Then, in the 11th, the Indians' Kenny Lofton (right and below, tumbling into his teammates' arms) singled and eventually scored on a hit by Jolbert Cabrera.

NO SUCH THING AS A FREE PASS: Atlanta's Greg Maddux broke the N.L. record for consecutive innings without allowing a base on balls—the mark of 68 had been shared by Christy Mathewson and Randy Jones—during a six-inning outing against the Astros on August 7. Five days later, Maddux extended his streak to 72 innings before being ordered to issue an intentional walk against Arizona.

GOING LIKE 60: The Cubs' Sammy Sosa, who had a three-homer game against the Rockies on August 9, repeated the long-ball salvo later in the year against the Brewers and the Astros. In addition to becoming the first player in major league history to hit three homers in a game three times in one season, Sosa set a big-league record with his third 60-homer year. He hit his 60th of the 2001 season against the Reds (opposite page, bottom left) and finished the year with 64 home runs and a career-high 160 runs batted in. Sosa had connected for 66 homers in the 1998 season and 63 in 1999.

CLIMBING UP TO #5: Mark McGwire, who began the season at No. 7 on the career home run list, passed Reggie Jackson in July, then vaulted ahead of Harmon Killebrew and into the No. 5 spot when he hit homer No. 574 on August 11 against the Mets. McGwire, who hit 29 homers in 97 games, announced his retirement after the 2001 season, finishing with 583 career home runs.

NEWCOMER TOSSES NO-HITTER:
St. Louis rookie Bud Smith's fourth major league victory was a memorable one—a stretch-run no-hitter against San Diego at Qualcomm Stadium. Smith had a high pitch count (inset) in his gem but persevered. The lefthander, who made a switch in uniform numbers during the season, was no stranger to no-hitters, having tossed two in the minor leagues in the 2000 season.

A COUPLE OF ACES: The Yankees' Roger Clemens (left) and Mike Mussina made big news in September, Clemens becoming the first big-league pitcher to reach the 20-victory plateau with only one loss and Mussina coming within one strike of pitching a perfect game. Defeating the White Sox on September 19 in Chicago, Clemens improved his record to 20-1 with his 16th consecutive win. Mussina, pitching at Fenway Park on September 2, retired the first 26 hitters he faced before the Red Sox's Carl Everett, on a count of 0-2, lined a single to left-center. Mussina (inset, following the flight of Everett's ball) then retired Trot Nixon, completing a one-hit, 1-0 triumph in which he struck out 13 batters.

Tragedy strikes

When terrorists attacked the United States on September 11 and inflicted unfathomable loss of life on its citizenry, reaction nationwide came in the form of shock, sadness, anger and fear.

It was a time for Americans to mourn, to reflect and to show steely resolve. It was not a time for athletic competition.

"The President, when I see him, kids me about the tough job I have," baseball commissioner Bud Selig said on that horrific Tuesday. "I guess if I were with him today, I'd say it might be a tough job but it's all about games. His job is tough, and it's about life and death. I can't worry about games today."

Accordingly, major league baseball was shut down until further notice. The "No Game Today" decision seemed only right.

In the days ahead, though, as the nation grieved and tried to find its way, it became clear that sports—big-league baseball, pro and college football and other athletic endeavors—would provide a much-needed diversion and some semblance of a return to normalcy in Americans' lives.

Selig and the rest of baseball's hierarchy proceeded to map plans for a resumption of play—and the commissioner gave the go-ahead. The date chosen was September 17, when six National League games would be played. The first game in New York, where the World Trade Center had collapsed after being rammed by two hijacked airliners, would be September 21 at Shea Stadium.

When the Cardinals and the Brewers met at Busch Stadium six days after the nation stood still, there was a patriotic fervor present that left fans and players teary-eyed (St. Louis' Bobby Bonilla, right, reacts to a video montage depicting American ideals). Flags were everywhere (including small ones stitched on players' uniforms), firefighters and police officers were honored, longtime Cardinals broadcaster Jack Buck read a poem he had a written and chants of "U-S-A! U-S-A! U-S-A!" reverberated throughout the stadium.

Similarly gripping scenes unfolded that night and in the coming days at other ballparks, with the most emotional ceremonies being held at Shea Stadium (where, below, fans showed their allegiance during a Mets-Braves series).

It was an emotional scene at Shea Stadium on the night of September 21 when baseball returned to New York. Flags were hoisted and eyes were dabbed, and Mets and Braves players—who had developed a fierce rivalry in recent years—embraced. Rick White, who was among Mets players wearing caps that honored rescue workers at the World Trade Center in lower Manhattan, had a warm meeting with Atlanta's Chipper Jones.

Shea Stadium's image of the New York skyline, with a ribbon placed in front of the twin towers of the World Trade Center, was a poignant sight for fans and players, who felt another emotional surge when Liza Minnelli sang a rousing rendition of "New York, New York" during the seventh-inning stretch. The Mets' Mike Piazza then stirred the crowd once more by hitting a game-winning home run in the eighth inning.

Baseball showed its colors—red, white and blue—when it resumed play. Flags were affixed to batting helmets, to the backs of uniforms, to sleeves and even to the bases, and a large ribbon—one honoring America and the victims of the September 11 attacks—stood out to the left of home plate at Shea Stadium, where the Mets and Joe McEwing (at bat) took on the Braves and Andruw Jones.

cap.com
new era cap.com
new era cap
47
Mets
31
USA

SENSATIONAL IN SEATTLE: The Mariners, who got big offensive contributions from Ichiro Suzuki, Bret Boone, Edgar Martinez, John Olerud and Mike Cameron, great starting pitching from Jamie Moyer, Freddy Garcia, Aaron Sele and Paul Abbott and stellar relief work from Kazuhiro Sasaki, Arthur Rhodes and Jeff Nelson, tied the major league mark for victories in a season, 116. They bolted to a 31-9 start, were 60-21 at the halfway point, got to 50 games over .500 on August 4 and 60 games over on September 5 and reached 71 games over the break-even mark (116-45) before losing their final game of the 2001 season.

ATHLETICS' ASCENT: After digging themselves into a hole in the A.L. West with an 8-18 start, the A's caught fire midway through the season and stormed to a wild-card playoff berth. With slugger Jason Giambi (left) and pitchers (top, left to right) Tim Hudson, Mark Mulder and Barry Zito leading the way, Oakland finished the year on a 61-17 surge and wound up with the second-best record in the majors (102-60).

73!

Sure, Barry Bonds had a record 39 home runs at the All-Star break. But he had been stuck on 39 for two weeks after an absolutely stunning 12-week power display, leaving more than a few critics to say that Bonds' attempt to break Mark McGwire's seemingly unassailable record of 70 homers in one season would fall way short.

After all, the thinking went, Bonds never had hit even 50 homers in a season, so if he reached anything close to 60, it would be amazing.

Bonds wasn't listening. He homered in his first game after the break, hit five more in July and then clubbed 12 in August, bringing his total to 57. No. 60 came on September 6 against Arizona, and Bonds then had the game that he later said made him think he had a real chance to top McGwire's record. On September 9 at Coors Field, he walloped three home runs. With three weeks left in the season, his total stood at 63.

Fate then intervened. The terrorist attacks on September 11 halted play in the majors for six days (longer for some teams), and it was difficult for players and fans to retain interest in on-field goings-on. Bonds put himself in that category.

After Bonds' big game in Denver, the Giants didn't play again until September 18. Bonds, somehow regaining his focus, homered two days later, then hit two in San Diego and one in Los Angeles. *Sixty-seven.*

Bonds clubbed Nos. 68 and 69 against San Diego on September 28-29, then took his quest for the record to Houston. After a walk fest for most of the three-game series, Bonds hit a ninth-inning homer in the third game to tie McGwire.

Record-breaking No. 71—and No. 72 as well—came on October 5 against the Dodgers. And the new major league homer record became 73 when Bonds homered on the last day of the season (right) against Los Angeles. He was greeted by his son Nikolai at home plate at Pacific Bell Park.

PACIFIC BELL
42
3
4
11
24
27
30
44
25
16
339

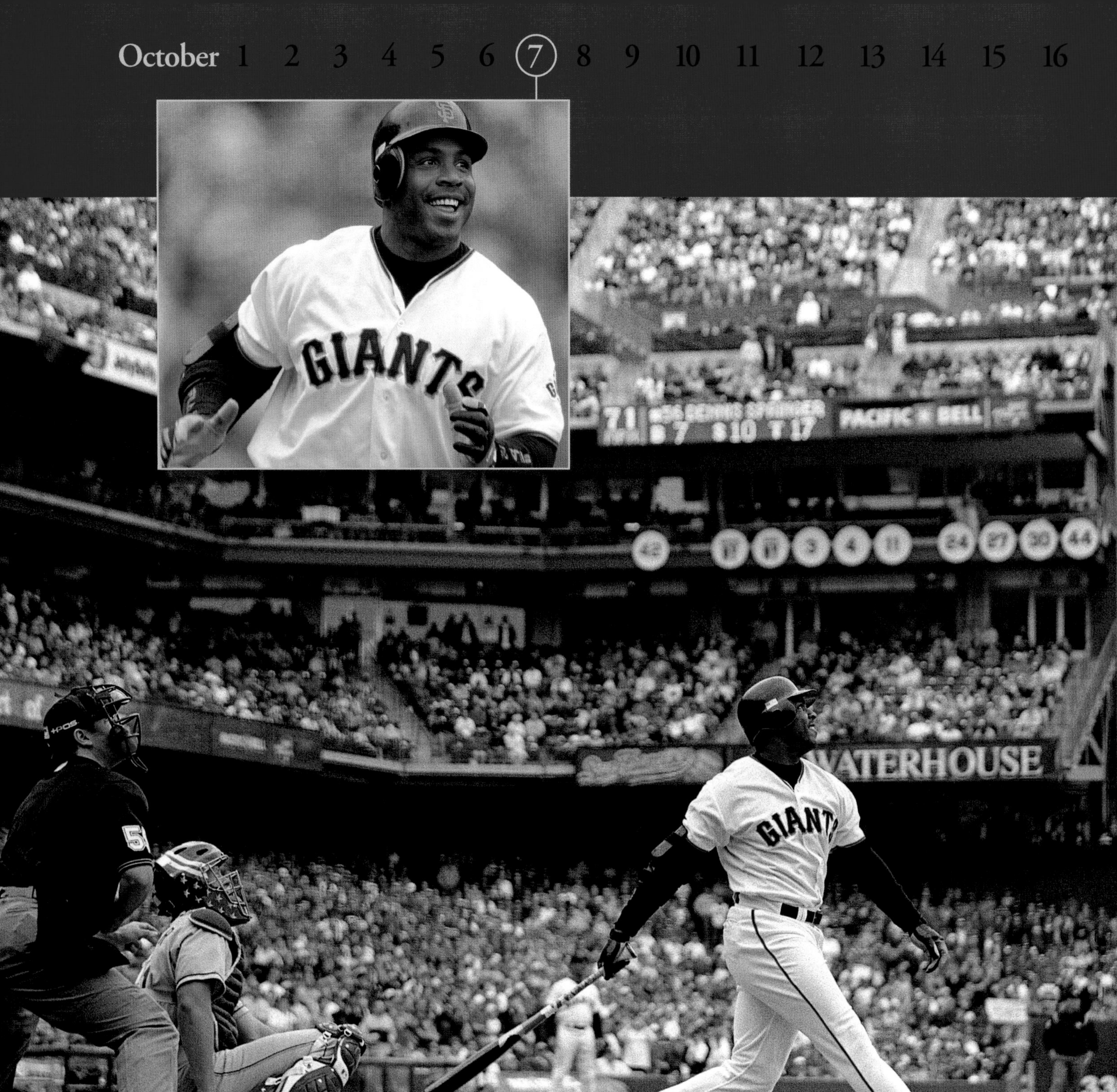

Bonds drilled home run No. 73 off the Dodgers' Dennis Springer, and he took special delight (above and inset) in connecting for the landmark shot off a knuckleball pitcher. "The chance of hitting a home run off a guy who throws that slow is slim," Bonds said. "I just said, 'What else can you give me, God?' " By day's end, Bonds had wrapped up a year in which he set big-league season records for home runs, walks (177) and slugging percentage (.863), the latter two marks previously held by Babe Ruth. Bonds also finished with a .328 batting average and a career-high 137 runs batted in.

Having tied the season homer mark in his final at-bat in Houston the night before, Bonds wasted little time in becoming the new king when he cut loose for No. 71 (left) in his first trip to the plate in the opening game of a season-ending series in San Francisco on October 5. The return to the dugout was a happy occasion for Bonds, who got the record-breaker against the archrival Los Angeles Dodgers.

SAN FRANCISCO
family

After drawing an intentional walk (below, left) in his previous at-bat with the Giants leading Houston, 8-1, on October 4—the base on balls was his eighth in the three-game series—Bonds crushed a ninth-inning pitch from rookie Wilfredo Rodriguez for his 70th home run. His arms raised triumphantly, Bonds watched his mammoth blow at Enron Field and then got a hero's welcome at the plate. The next night in San Francisco, Bonds smashed No. 71, a first-inning blast off Los Angeles' Chan Ho Park, and was honored in a ceremony (below, right), alongside his godfather, Giants legend and Hall of Famer Willie Mays. Bonds connected for No. 72 in the third inning, also against Park.

A BIG FINISH FOR RICKEY:
Three days after breaking Ty Cobb's career runs record, Rickey Henderson got his 3,000th hit (and an award to note the feat, right) in the Padres' last game of the year. When he set the runs record with a home run, Henderson slid into home and then received a gold plaque of the plate. Earlier in the year, he broke Babe Ruth's career walks mark at Shea Stadium.

SO LONG: Cal Ripken and Tony Gwynn said their goodbyes on October 6 and October 7, respectively, in games at Camden Yards and Qualcomm Stadium. The Orioles' Ripken, who went 0-for-3 against the Red Sox, was in the on-deck circle when the final game of his career ended. Gwynn, sent up as a pinch hitter for the Padres in the ninth inning of a game against the Rockies, grounded out in his last at-bat.

STEPS DOWN: Shortly after the end of the regular season, Tom Kelly announced he was retiring as manager of the Twins. Kelly, who had led Minnesota to World Series titles in 1987 and 1991, found considerable satisfaction in keeping the low-payroll Twins in contention in 2001 after hearing critics claim "the game had passed him by." Minnesota led the A.L. Central at the All-Star break and finished in second place.

2001 POSTSEASON

DIVISION
SERIES
2001

DOMINANT: Arizona righthander Curt Schilling received all the run support he needed when Steve Finley delivered a fifth-inning single that scored Damian Miller. Schilling recorded nine strikeouts in the opener of the Division Series.

2001 NATIONAL LEAGUE DIVISION SERIES, GAME 1

Diamondbacks 1 Cardinals 0

Schilling sizzles in the desert

It was a classic matchup of the major league season's two winningest pitchers, veteran Curt Schilling and fourth-year man Matt Morris.

The veteran won out. Barely.

Arizona's Schilling, coming off a 22-6 record in his 14th year in the big leagues, outdueled Morris by tossing a three-hitter as the Diamondbacks won Game 1 of the Division Series with the Cardinals, 1-0, at Bank One Ballpark in Phoenix.

Morris, who in April 1999 underwent major elbow surgery and made a remarkable comeback by going 22-8 in 2001, allowed only six hits in seven innings but was touched for a game-deciding run in the fifth inning.

After Morris wriggled out of a first-inning jam—the Diamondbacks had runners on second and third base and no one out—he and Schilling matched zeros until Arizona's Damian Miller was hit by a pitch to lead off the fifth, moved to second on a sacrifice by Schilling and, one out later, scored on Steve Finley's single to center.

Schilling walked only one batter and struck out nine while pitching his second consecutive shutout in postseason play. In his last October start, he had blanked Toronto in Game 5 of the 1993 World Series.

St. Louis got two hits from Edgar Renteria and a spectacular catch by center fielder Jim Edmonds, but the Cards' offense couldn't break through against Schilling.

2001 NATIONAL LEAGUE DIVISION SERIES, GAME 2

Cardinals 4 Diamondbacks 1

A HEAD-SCRATCHER: After losing for the seventh consecutive time in postseason play, Randy Johnson was at a loss to explain his misfortune to the media. Johnson pitched well against St. Louis, allowing six hits and three runs in eight innings and striking out nine. The Diamondbacks' fate was sealed when Cardinals reliever Steve Kline retired Matt Williams on a ninth-inning groundout and pumped his fist in victory.

Williams, Pujols deliver for Cards

When the Cardinals obtained righthander Woody Williams from San Diego with two months remaining in the regular season, it hardly seemed like a make-or-break transaction. But Williams, at age 35, proceeded to dazzle, posting a 7-1 record and a 2.28 ERA for St. Louis and helping the Cardinals spurt into the playoffs as a wild-card entry.

It made sense, then, that manager Tony La Russa had enough confidence in the gritty Williams to start him against Arizona with the Cards down by one game in the Division Series. And Williams came up big, pitching seven-plus innings of four-hit ball in a 4-1 Cardinals victory.

Not only did Williams deliver in a crucial game in the best-of-five series, but he beat 21-game winner Randy Johnson in the process. Johnson, who somehow had lost six consecutive postseason decisions entering this game, led the N.L. in strikeouts (372) and ERA (2.49) in the 2001 season.

The Cards jumped on Johnson in the the first inning, with rookie sensation Albert Pujols connecting for a two-run homer. They added single runs in the third and ninth, and reliever Steve Kline shut down Arizona after the D-backs struck for a run in the eighth.

2001 NATIONAL LEAGUE DIVISION SERIES, GAME 3

Diamondbacks 5 Cardinals 3

DECISIVE BLOW: Craig Counsell's three-run homer highlighted the Diamondbacks' four-run, seventh-inning outburst.

An unlikely hero for Arizona

The Diamondbacks had some muscle on their roster—namely, Luis Gonzalez, Reggie Sanders, Matt Williams and Steve Finley. So when they won Game 3 with the long ball, it wasn't a shock. But when the lethal blow came off the bat off Craig Counsell, the Busch Stadium crowd could scarcely believe it.

Nor could St. Louis fans believe that manager Tony La Russa stuck with journeyman lefthanded reliever Mike Matthews as long as he did in the fateful seventh inning.

Down by a 2-1 score against Darryl Kile entering the seventh, Arizona got a leadoff walk—at which point La Russa removed Kile in favor of Matthews. After a force play, Damian Miller and pinch hitter Greg Colbrunn followed with singles that enabled the Diamondbacks to tie the game. One out later, Counsell, who had only four homers and 29 extra-base hits during the season, cracked a three-run homer to right off Matthews.

The Cardinals, after closing the gap to 5-3 on an Edgar Renteria homer in their half of the seventh, failed to cash in on a bases-loaded opportunity in the eighth. Then, in the ninth, their first two batters reached base against reliever Byung-Hyun Kim, but Mike Matheny struck out after fouling off two bunt attempts and Mark McGwire, in a pinch-hitting role, grounded into a double play.

2001 N.L. DIVISION SERIES, GAME 4

Cardinals 4 Diamondbacks 1

Rookie justifies La Russa's faith

Bud Smith had made all of 14 starts for the Cardinals in the regular season, but manager Tony La Russa had no qualms about giving the rookie the ball to start Game 4 of the Division Series against the Diamondbacks.

Smith didn't disappoint.

In a win-or-else situation for St. Louis, Smith permitted only one run and four hits over five innings before giving way to Dustin Hermanson, normally a starter, who pitched three perfect innings, and Steve Kline.

Fernando Vina hit a two-run homer for the Cards and went 3-for-3, and Jim Edmonds homered and continued his strong defensive play in center field in a game whose start was delayed more than 3½ hours because of rain.

Albie Lopez, obtained in a late-July trade to shore up Arizona's rotation, was the D-backs' starter and loser.

FLEXING HIS MUSCLES: St. Louis center fielder Jim Edmonds, who had homered in Game 3 against the D-backs, went deep again in Game 4 when he drove an Albie Lopez pitch over the wall in left-center. Luis Gonzalez did his best to corral the ball but was left hanging.

2001 NATIONAL LEAGUE DIVISION SERIES, GAME 5

Diamondbacks 2 Cardinals 1

The Schilling/Womack show

TONY-ON-THE-SPOT: The Diamondbacks' Tony Womack made a third-inning error (right) and failed to execute a ninth-inning suicide squeeze, but he followed the botched bunt attempt with a game-winning single (above) that scored pinch runner Danny Bautista, whose arrival at the plate got a hearty approval from teammate Craig Counsell.

They went at it again. This time, a berth in the N.L. Championship Series was at stake.

Curt Schilling vs. Matt Morris, the rematch. Could they possibly equal their sterling performances in Game 1? Not likely.

But it was close.

Schilling, backed by a bases-empty, fourth-inning home run by Reggie Sanders, took a 1-0 lead into the eighth inning but yielded a two-out homer to J.D. Drew. Then, in the ninth, he allowed a leadoff single to Jim Edmonds. Kerry Robinson, a good bunter, was sent up as a pinch hitter for Mark McGwire and sacrificed Edmonds to second. With the go-ahead run in scoring position, Schilling proceeded to strike out Edgar Renteria and Mike Matheny.

Morris gave way to Dave Veres in the D-backs' ninth, and Matt Williams greeted him with a double. After a sacrifice and an intentional walk (issued by new reliever Steve Kline), Tony Womack failed to make contact on a suicide squeeze and pinch runner Midre Cummings was thrown out at the plate. But Womack redeemed himself by blooping a run-scoring hit to left field.

The D-backs were NLCS-bound.

2001 AMERICAN LEAGUE DIVISION SERIES, GAME 1

A's 5 Yankees 3

A's get the jump on the Rocket

The Oakland A's rolled into New York as the wild-card entrant in the playoffs, but also as the hottest team in baseball and the team with the best record in the second half of the season.

They also rolled in wanting to make amends for last year, when they lost to the Yankees in a five-game Division Series.

The opener featured a matchup that mirrored the contrast in the two teams: Oakland, the young and brash A's, opened with 24-year-old lefthander Mark Mulder; New York, the veteran and steady Yankees, opened with 39-year-old righthander Roger Clemens.

Just as it was last year, the A's beat Clemens in the opener. After an emotional pregame ceremony that honored the relief workers dedicated to working amid the ruins of the terrorist attacks in New York City, Oakland started fast. The A's touched Clemens for a run in the first, breaking Clemens' 17-game postseason scoreless string, with the help of one of its offseason acquisitions, Johnny Damon, who wound up 4-for-4. The A's also displayed their power: Terrence Long homered twice in the game and Jason Giambi hit another.

Mulder was the model of composure, surviving a first-inning Yankees threat. He threw 6⅔ innings, striking out five and allowing only seven hits. Relievers Jim Mecir and Jason Isringhausen closed it out.

YANKEE KILLERS: Mark Mulder (right), coming off an A.L.-leading 21 victories in the regular season, got key offensive support from Terrence Long (above), who homered twice in the game, and won his matchup with Roger Clemens.

TROUBLE IN GOTHAM: Oakland's Tim Hudson (left) pitched eight scoreless innings against New York and closer Jason Isringhausen finished the job, putting the Yankees on the brink of elimination. The Yanks managed only seven hits—two of them by Derek Jeter, who was forced out at second base (below) in the first inning (with Frank Menechino making the play for the A's).

2001 AMERICAN LEAGUE DIVISION SERIES, GAME 2

A's 2 Yankees 0

Hudson throttles Yanks

If Game 2 wasn't a must-win situation for the Yankees, it was as close as it was going to get. A loss in the opener meant the Yankees would have to win one of two games in Oakland's Network Associates Coliseum, where the A's had held a decided home advantage in the second half of the season.

A loss in Game 2 would mean the Yanks would have to take two in hostile territory to bring the series back to New York for a Game 5.

But even with playoff ace Andy Pettitte, who had compiled a 6-1 postseason record from 1998 through 2000, pitching in Game 2, the Yankees couldn't get it done—mostly because they couldn't solve Oakland's Tim Hudson. Veteran Ron Gant staked the A's to a 1-0 lead with a fourth-inning homer, and they added a run in the ninth inning.

The Yankees' offense stirred in their ninth. Bernie Williams led off with a double and Tino Martinez walked. But Jorge Posada struck out and David Justice and Scott Brosius popped out, and the Yanks were headed to Oakland one loss away from elimination.

2001 AMERICAN LEAGUE DIVISION SERIES, GAME 3

Yankees 1 A's 0

It's Derek Jeter to the rescue

Defense, the thinking goes, wins championships. In a one-run game, it can take one play—one defensive stop—to make the difference.

In Game 3, it was one defensive play that turned the game and provided the Yankees with some energy and, perhaps more important, momentum.

Not surprisingly, the big play came from shortstop Derek Jeter. Ahead 1-0 thanks to a Jorge Posada home run, the Yankees were trying to fight off the A's in the seventh inning. With Jeremy Giambi on first base and two out, Terrence Long doubled to right. As Giambi was waved home, Jeter fielded a throw from Shane Spencer halfway up the first-base line—Spencer had missed the cutoff man—and, in a single, graceful motion, flipped the ball sidearm to catcher Posada, who grazed Giambi at the plate.

"That's just pure instinct," said Oakland's Johnny Damon. "That's why Derek is such a great shortstop. No other shortstop is backing up that play there. ..."

HEADS UP: Derek Jeter's corralling of a throw down the first-base line and his quick flip to the plate nailed Jeremy Giambi.

MAKING IT LOOK EASY: By the time Bernie Williams scored a ninth-inning run for the Yankees, the New Yorkers had turned Game 4 into a laugher. Williams had a lot to do with the one-sided nature of the Division Series-squaring game, going 3-for-4 with five RBIs. The victory came the day after Mike Mussina had pitched seven shutout innings in a tense Yankees win.

2001 AMERICAN LEAGUE DIVISION SERIES, GAME 4

Yankees 9 A's 2

Big 'Mo' fuels Yankees' surge

Still one game, one loss from elimination, the Yankees carried their momentum from Game 3 into Game 4—and kept rolling. Rolling enough to pound out a 9-2 victory, and rolling enough to push the Division Series back to where the Yankees wanted it: home in the Bronx.

This time, the Yankees' heroes were El Duque, Orlando Hernandez, who had struggled mightily during the regular season, and center fielder Bernie Williams. With postseason experience on his side, Hernandez pitched well enough to win in a 5⅔-innings stint and received more than the offensive support he needed.

What Hernandez did on the mound, Williams did at the plate. Williams drove in five runs, two on a double in the third, two on a single in the fourth and another on a double in the ninth.

With a rested bullpen, an emotional home crowd waiting and Roger Clemens going in decisive Game 5, the Yankees liked their chances of advancing to the American League Championship Series.

2001 A.L. DIVISION SERIES, GAME 5

Yankees 5 A's 3

The Yankees: just too much—again

In the end, it was too much Yankees experience, too much Roger Clemens and Derek Jeter, too much David Justice and Mariano Rivera—just too much for Oakland to handle in the fifth and final game of the Division Series.

Clemens, who struggled but turned in a gritty performance, got the Yankees to their middle relievers—Mike Stanton and Ramiro Mendoza.

Rivera then showed, again, why he's the best closer in the league, shutting down the A's offense.

Justice struggled in this series, but the veteran hit a key pinch home run.

And then there was Jeter, who embodied the Yankees' resolve by diving into the photographers' well to snare Terrence Long's foul ball.

Having beaten the hottest team in baseball, New York now faced the prospect of playing the team that had tied the major league record for victories in a season, the Seattle Mariners, in the ALCS. A daunting task, yes, but the Yankees were still baseball's champions—until proved otherwise.

NEXT UP, THE ALCS: After Roger Clemens hit Oakland's Miguel Tejada with a fifth-inning pitch (opposite page) in Game 5, Yankees manager Joe Torre went to his bullpen. No matter. New York's relief corps pitched $4\frac{2}{3}$ innings of scoreless ball and, aided by a sixth-inning home run by David Justice (middle photo), helped the Yankees to a familiar celebratory scene at game's end.

2001 N.L. CHAMPIONSHIP SERIES, GAME 1

Diamondbacks 2 Braves 0

'Gorilla' is off Johnson's back

Addressing the media after the game, Arizona's Randy Johnson was ready: "Assuming someone might say, 'Is this a monkey off your back?' ... This is more like a gorilla."

Johnson had just tossed a three-hit shutout against Atlanta in Game 1 of the N.L. Championship Series, ending a personal seven-game postseason losing streak. Johnson struck out 11 batters, walked only one and retired 20 consecutive Braves in one stretch.

Not that it didn't get interesting. Guarding a 2-0 lead with two out and none on in the ninth inning, Johnson allowed singles to Julio Franco and Chipper Jones. Brian Jordan, who got key hits for Atlanta time and again in 2001, was up next and posed a major threat, but Johnson reached back and struck him out.

Craig Counsell singled and doubled off Greg Maddux and scored both Arizona runs.

Atlanta suffered its first 2001 postseason loss, having swept Houston in the Division Series.

BRAVES NOT SO CHIPPER: Randy Johnson frustrated (left) could attest. Craig Counsell was Arizona's offensive spark,

the Braves throughout Game 1, as strikeout victim Chipper Jones stroking a first-inning single and a fifth-inning double (above).

2001 NATIONAL LEAGUE CHAMPIONSHIP SERIES, GAME 2

Braves 8 Diamondbacks 1

Lopez, Glavine knot the series

Catcher Javy Lopez, sidelined for the last week of the regular season because of an ankle injury and relegated to one pinch-hitting appearance in the first four games of Atlanta's postseason run, was penciled into the lineup for Game 2 of the NLCS in hopes of providing an offensive spark for the Braves.

Consider it mission accomplished.

With Tom Glavine and the Diamondbacks' Miguel Batista locked in a 1-1 pitching duel, Lopez delivered the game's decisive blow when he drilled a two-run homer in the seventh. In the eighth, Brian Jordan's two-run double and B.J. Surhoff's two-run homer featured a five-run Braves outburst.

Glavine, who had pitched eight shutout innings against Houston in Game 2 of the Division Series, hurled five-hit ball over seven innings against the Diamondbacks.

"Tom Glavine was every bit as spectacular in his own right as Randy Johnson was (in Game 1), if you ask me," Diamondbacks manager Bob Brenly said. "He pitched right to the strength of his defense. That's pretty crafty."

Glavine said he "always thought Game 2 is an urgent game in any series. To me, it's a huge swing. We certainly didn't want to go home down 2-0 with the prospect of facing Curt (Schilling)."

SLUMBER ENDS: The Braves, held scoreless in Game 1 of the National League Championship Series, hit three home runs in Game 2—the last coming off the bat of B.J. Surhoff, who connected for an eighth-inning shot off Arizona reliever Greg Swindell.

IT MIGHT BE ... IT COULD BE: Atlanta's Javy Lopez watched his seventh-inning smash off Miguel Batista (left) sail over the wall for a two-run homer. Batista pitched well in his matchup with Tom Glavine, allowing only two hits over seven innings—but both of those hits were home runs (the other coming off the bat of Marcus Giles).

2001 N.L. CHAMPIONSHIP SERIES, GAME 3

Diamondbacks 5 Braves 1

Schilling continues scintillating pace

After two marvelous performances in the Division Series, it was hard to imagine what Arizona's Curt Schilling had up his sleeve this time around.

A four-hit, 12-strikeout effort, that's what. And his third complete game of the 2001 postseason. It was easily enough to propel the Diamondbacks to a two-games-to-one lead over the Braves.

"I've never thrown better in more important games—I think it's pretty obvious," acknowledged Schilling, whose strikeout total stood at 30 after 27 innings of postseason pitching.

Schilling also was a factor on offense, igniting a three-run Arizona outburst in the fifth inning with a single and later scoring on a error. He bowled over catcher Javy Lopez on the play, allowing another run to score.

Diamondbacks center fielder Steve Finley doubled home two runs in the third and singled in a run in the fifth. Craig Counsell went 3-for-4 for Arizona.

Atlanta threw everything it could at the D-backs, employing seven pitchers. But starter John Burkett allowed too much damage—he was charged with all five Arizona runs.

HERE'S YOUR RUN SUPPORT: A two-run double in the third inning by Steve Finley (left, bottom) provided all the offense Curt Schilling really needed in Game 3. Craig Counsell (left, top) had three singles for Arizona in its win at Turner Field.

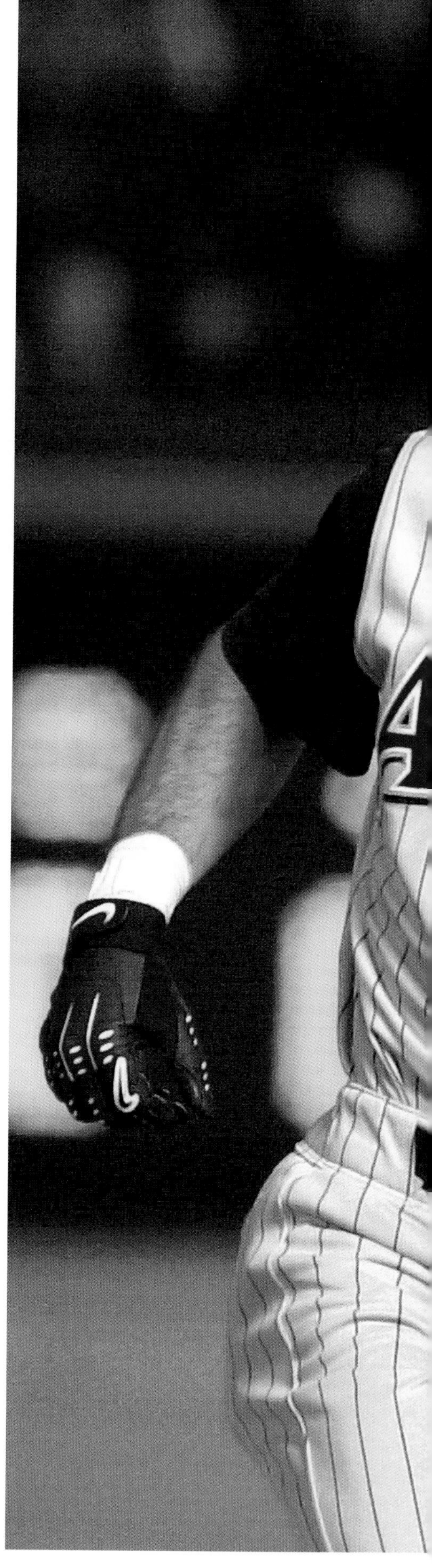

2001 N.L. CHAMPIONSHIP SERIES, GAME 4

Diamondbacks 11 Braves 4

Maddux's pitching and fielding unravel

Pitching on only three days' rest, Atlanta ace Greg Maddux (above) was, well, just awful. And the Braves' defense stunk up the joint, too, making three errors in one inning (one of them by Maddux) and four overall.

By game's end, Arizona had six unearned runs—and an easy victory that pulled the Diamondbacks within one triumph of the World Series.

Maddux, whose career NLCS record fell to 4-8, was shelled for eight hits in three innings-plus. By the time he left the game, the Braves had dug themselves a 6-2 hole.

Usually outstanding with the glove, Maddux was indecisive on a ball hit back to the mound, creating a bases-loaded situation in the third inning. He made a bad throw on a subsequent play as the Braves unraveled.

Arizona not only took advantage of Atlanta's shoddy defense, it also collected 12 hits—including three by Craig Counsell, who drove in four runs. Luis Gonzalez, coming off a 57-homer season, slugged a three-run home run in the ninth to seal the Braves' fate.

SOLID 1-2 PUNCH: Craig Counsell (sliding into home plate) and Luis Gonzalez (left, rounding the bases after a home run) combined for five hits and seven RBIs in Game 4, a contest in which each team used six pitchers. Byung-Hyun Kim closed out the Braves by getting the final six outs.

A TICKET TO THE FALL CLASSIC: A two-run home run by Erubiel Durazo (above) and the pitching of Randy Johnson and Byung-Hyun Kim vaulted the Diamondbacks into the World Series—an accomplishment in which Arizona players exulted.

2001 N.L. CHAMPIONSHIP SERIES, GAME 5

Diamondbacks 3 Braves 2

In fourth year, D-backs reach the World Series

A young franchise whose roster was dotted with thirtysomething players, the Arizona Diamondbacks roared into the World Series in spectacular fashion by dispatching the Atlanta Braves in five games in the NLCS.

The most spectacular moment in this game came in the seventh inning when Arizona's Randy Johnson, trying to protect a 3-2 lead, struck out Brian Jordan with the bases loaded. D-backs manager Bob Brenly then turned the pitching chores over to Byung-Hyun Kim for the final two innings, and Kim kept the Atlanta bats in check.

Erubiel Durazo, pinch-hitting for an injured Mark Grace, delivered the game's deciding blow when he hit a two-run homer in the fifth off Tom Glavine. The Braves again were hurt by their defense, with Arizona's first batter of the inning reaching base on an error.

The D-backs, in only their fourth year of existence, were headed to the Fall Classic sparked by a 30-and-over gang whose members included Johnson, Grace, Curt Schilling, Luis Gonzalez, Craig Counsell (the NLCS MVP), Tony Womack, Matt Williams, Steve Finley, Reggie Sanders, Jay Bell, Damian Miller, Greg Colbrunn, Miguel Batista, Greg Swindell and Mike Morgan.

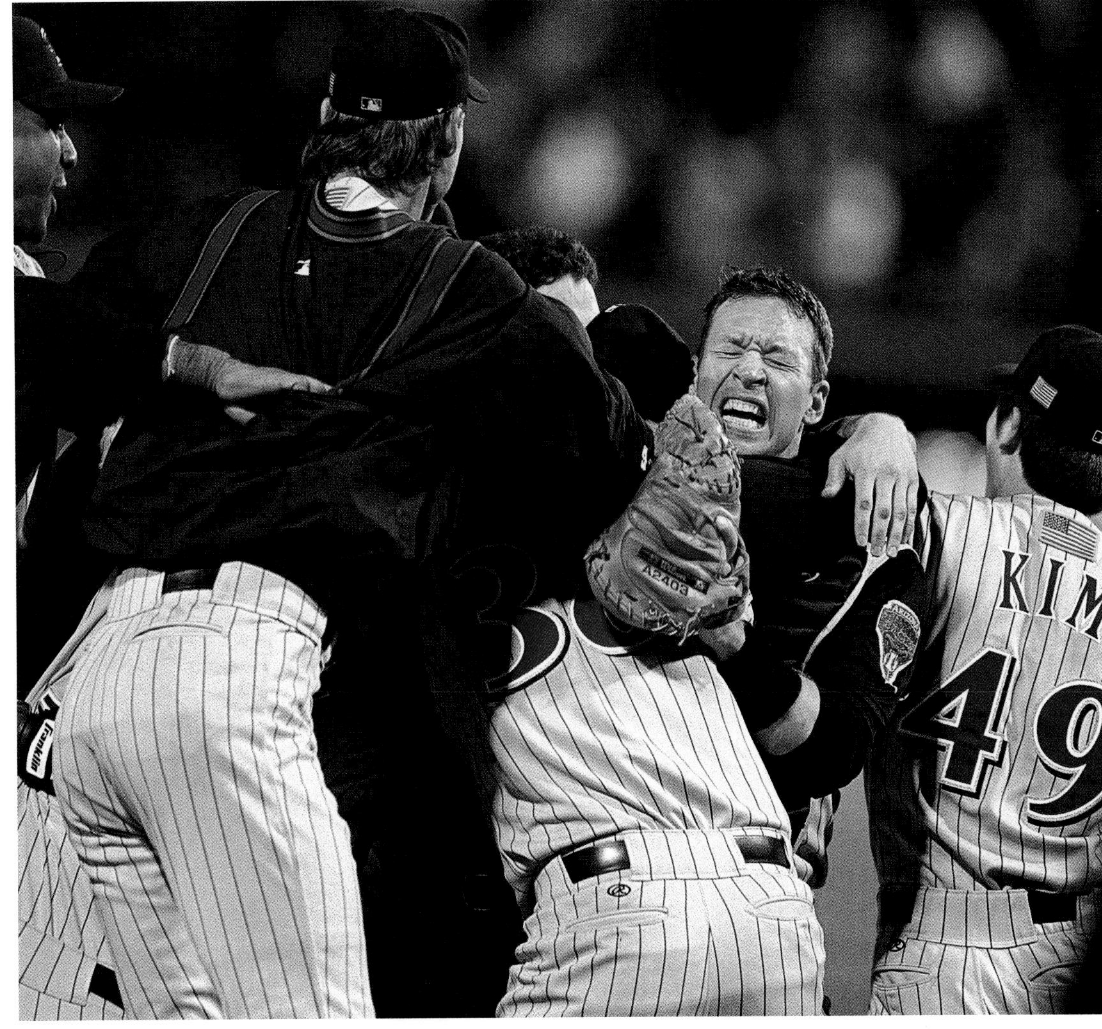

ANDY IS DANDY: Lefthander Andy Pettitte was locked in during the opener of the American League Championship Series, holding the Mariners hitless through four innings and striking out seven batters in an eight-inning outing. Pettitte improved his career ALCS record to 4-1.

2001 AMERICAN LEAGUE CHAMPIONSHIP SERIES, GAME 1

Yankees 4 Mariners 2

Experience prevails in opener

It was the matchup everyone had been eagerly awaiting: the New York Yankees vs. the Seattle Mariners. The defending World Series champions against the team with the best record in baseball in 2001.

And In just one game, the Yankees took away everything the Mariners had earned in their record-tying season of 116 wins. Behind playoff ace Andy Pettitte, and sparked by a two-run homer from veteran Paul O'Neill, the Yanks erased Seattle's home-field advantage and served notice that they were on a quest for another World Series crown.

Pettitte, who was 0-2 against the Mariners during the season, nonetheless allowed just three hits, none until the fifth inning. Mariano Rivera finished it, allowing a run in the ninth but still recording the save.

In the end, it came down to the Yankees' postseason experience and the lack of experience for the Mariners, who were coming off a 3-2 Division Series triumph over Cleveland.

"We're used to playing big games," O'Neill said. "We've got jitters and nerves like everybody else. But when we take the field, we've been successful."

SAFE AT HOME: Jorge Posada walked and doubled and scored twice in Game 1 for the Yankees, who played with their usual savvy and confidence against a Mariners team that had tied a major league record with 116 victories during the regular season.

2001 AMERICAN LEAGUE CHAMPIONSHIP SERIES, GAME 2

Yankees 3 Mariners 2

Yanks halfway home to Series

All of a sudden, a Yankees team that had looked all but dead after two games of its Division Series against Oakland was halfway to a familiar place: a spot in the World Series.

This time, New York's heroes were Mike Mussina, who gave up just four hits over six innings while outdueling Seattle's Freddy Garcia, and Scott Brosius. It was Brosius' two-run double in the second inning that got the Yankees up early. Mussina, coming off a big win in the ALDS, was guarding a 3-2 lead when he gave way to Ramiro Mendoza and Mariano Rivera.

In the first two games of the series at Safeco Field, Seattle had scored four runs and managed just 10 hits. The Mariners had gone hitless all 10 times with runners in scoring position and were just 6-for-46 in such situations in the entire postseason.

Still, down 0-2 and headed to New York, Seattle manager Lou Piniella was far from offering a concession speech.

"We're going to be back here to play Game 6," he vowed. "We've gone to New York and beaten this team five of six times (in the 2001 regular season) and we're going to do it again."

HALT: Ichiro Suzuki, the Mariners' season-long catalyst, reached base on a single, an error and an intentional walk in Game 2 but failed to score against the Yankees, who got strong pitching from Mike Mussina (opposite page), Ramiro Mendoza and Mariano Rivera. Stan Javier (inset) accounted for Seattle's runs with a homer.

YORK

LONG BALL: Just after reliever Mike Stanton (above, right) was removed from the game, Bret Boone hit a two-run homer off Mark Wohlers to cap a seven-run Mariners explosion in the sixth inning. Mark McLemore's bases-loaded triple was the big blow.

Mariners 14 Yankees 3

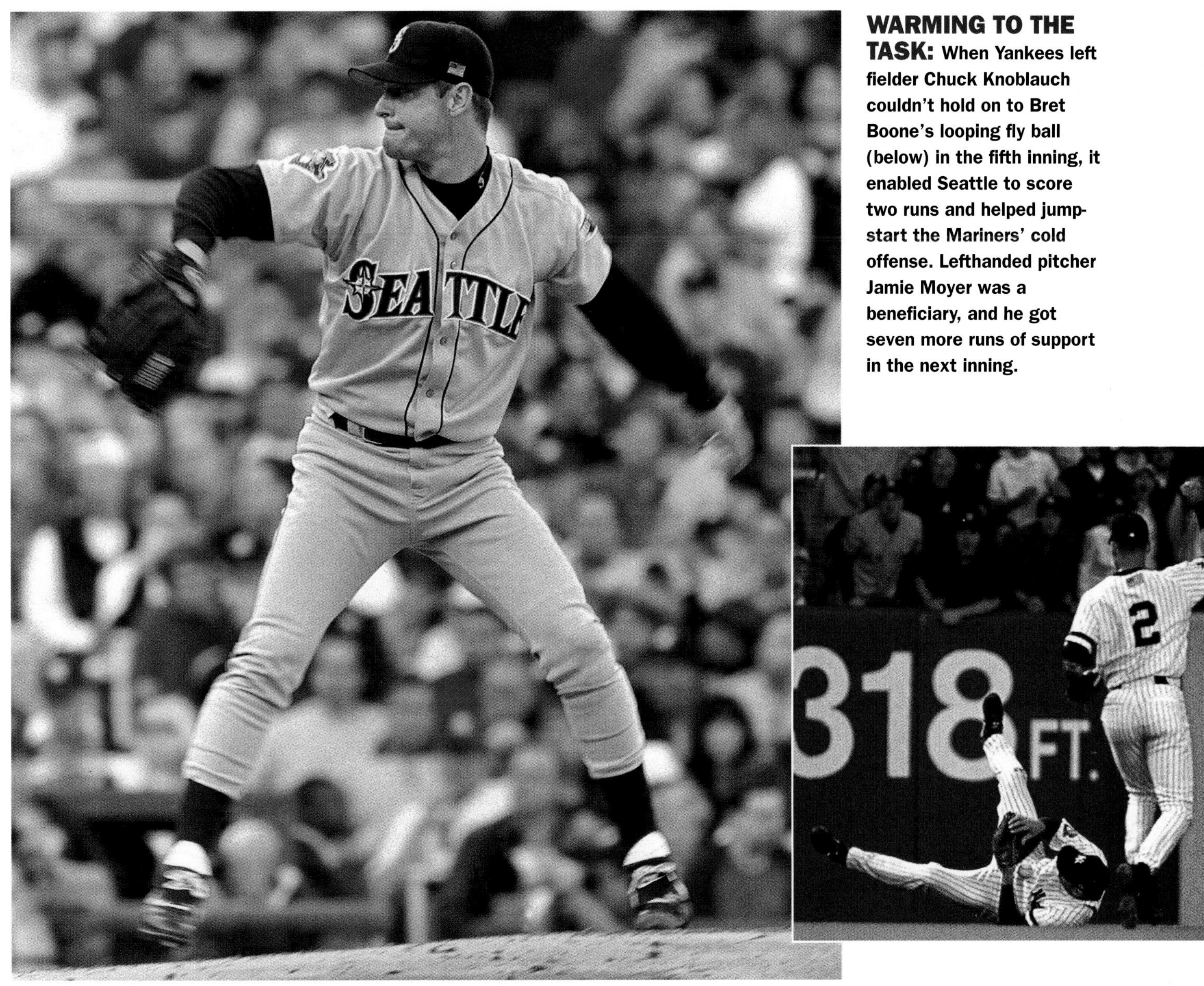

WARMING TO THE TASK: When Yankees left fielder Chuck Knoblauch couldn't hold on to Bret Boone's looping fly ball (below) in the fifth inning, it enabled Seattle to score two runs and helped jump-start the Mariners' cold offense. Lefthanded pitcher Jamie Moyer was a beneficiary, and he got seven more runs of support in the next inning.

Seattle's sleepy bats wake up

The Mariners' offense, dormant not just in this series but in the entire postseason, woke up for 14 runs, beating Orlando "El Duque" Hernandez and the Yankees in the first of three scheduled games at Yankee Stadium.

It was Jamie Moyer, a 20-game winner for the first time in his career, who won the big game for the Mariners. A loss would have meant an almost insurmountable 3-0 lead for New York in the League Championship Series. Seattle did it the hard way, quickly falling behind 2-0 and trailing by that margin heading into the fifth inning.

After a two-run homer in the first by the Yankees' Bernie Williams, Hernandez shut down Seattle until the fifth. Then the Seattle offense snapped out of its slumber. Bret Boone finally broke through for the Mariners—he would drive in five runs in the game—with a two-run single that fell out of Chuck Knoblauch's glove and the Seattle onslaught was on.

Another bit of good news for Seattle was the ineffectiveness of the Yankees' bullpen. The Mariners scored nine runs against relievers Mike Stanton, Mark Wohlers and Jay Witasick and moved within one victory of fulfilling manager Lou Piniella's promise to send the series back to Seattle.

2001 AMERICAN LEAGUE CHAMPIONSHIP SERIES, GAME 4

Yankees 3 Mariners 1

Young Yankee steps up as hero

This time, the hero was a youngster.

Buoyed by their cast of veterans throughout the postseason, the Yankees got the decisive offensive contribution in Game 4 from rookie second baseman Alfonso Soriano.

Facing Mariners closer Kazuhiro Sasaki in the ninth inning, Soriano drilled a two-run homer to bring the Yankees within a game of another World Series berth.

Staked to a 1-0 lead on an eighth-inning home run by Bret Boone, the Mariners gave back the run in the bottom half of the inning when Bernie Williams homered.

"There's a certain amount of magic that's tied to him," Yankees manager Joe Torre said of Williams. "We all expect it, and he's never let us down."

Mariano Rivera came on to shut down Seattle in the ninth. Scott Brosius then managed an infield single in the last half of the inning and Soriano unloaded into the bleachers in right-center.

The game featured a matchup of Roger Clemens and Paul Abbott. Abbott allowed no hits in five innings, but he walked eight batters and Seattle manager Lou Piniella went to his bullpen in the sixth.

A victory in Game 5 would enable the Yankees to avoid a return trip to Seattle. "We don't want to go back," Derek Jeter emphasized.

SHORT-LIVED: An eighth-inning home run by Bret Boone (immediate left) gave the Mariners the upper hand in Game 4, but only briefly. New York's Bernie Williams answered with a tying shot in New York's half of the inning, then Alfonso Soriano (opposite page) ended matters with a ninth-inning homer.

2001 A.L. CHAMPIONSHIP SERIES, GAME 5

Yankees 12 Mariners 3

Gritty Yankees advance

The Yankees earned a fourth consecutive trip to the World Series as New York's offense jumped on Aaron Sele and Andy Pettitte lived up to his postseason reputation.

"This ballclub will be remembered by me forever," said manager Joe Torre, who told his team: "Down 2-0 to one of the best clubs in baseball (the A's, in the Division Series), you never, never, never doubted yourselves."

Veterans Paul O'Neill, Tino Martinez and Bernie Williams homered for the Yankees. The defense came up with shoestring catches—left fielder Chuck Knoblauch thwarted a rally in the first inning with such a grab, and a sliding catch by right fielder Shane Spencer ended the game.

The Mariners' defense was shaky and their offense struggled against Pettitte, who had won the opener of this series.

"To get to this point is very gratifying," Martinez said. "The city's gone through a lot, the country's gone through a lot, but mainly the city. We try to represent New York City well."

The Yankees scored four runs in the third off Sele, two on a homer by Williams, and forced the Mariners to try to play catch-up again. "We got some huge two-out hits in that inning," Scott Brosius said, "and that's how you win games."

PINSTRIPE RITUAL: Getting major contributions in Game 5 from their veteran players, including pitcher Andy Pettitte (opposite page), the New York Yankees again were headed to the World Series.

2001 World Series

WHEEL OF FORTUNE
3

AMERICA WEST
AIRLINES

COX

A2000

2001 WORLD SERIES, GAME 1

Diamondbacks 9 Yankees 1

Another postseason game ... and another gem for Schilling

The Great Curt Schilling Postseason Show continued on baseball's greatest stage—the World Series.

Throwing big-time heat in the desert, Schilling made the Arizona Diamondbacks' first World Series game a memorable one by pitching three-hit ball over seven innings and striking out eight Yankees. The D-backs romped, thanks to Schilling's standout effort, timely hitting and a shaky New York defense.

Schilling, who improved his 2001 postseason record to 4-0, got key offensive support from Craig Counsell, who staked him to a first-inning lead with a home run; Luis Gonzalez, who hit a two-run homer in Arizona's four-run spree in the third inning; and Mark Grace, who contributed a two-run double in another four-run D-backs outburst, this one coming in the fourth inning.

Two New York errors helped Arizona cash in for five unearned runs at Bank One Ballpark in Phoenix. Mike Mussina, who had won 17 games for the Yankees in the regular season and pitched magnificently against Oakland in Game 3 of the Division Series, lasted only three innings. He gave up six hits—including both Arizona home runs—and five runs (three earned).

"The Yankees are who they are," Schilling said, "but that doesn't mean they are going to beat us. We have a job to do and we deserve to be here, just like they deserve to be here."

Added a prescient Schilling: "I feel real good I didn't throw a lot of pitches (102) tonight. If I have to come back on three days' rest, I'll be ready."

REMEMBERING: The World Series opener was on October 27, but there clearly was another date on everyone's mind when Bank One Ballpark in Phoenix played host to Game 1. Amid a patriotic atmosphere, Arizona and Curt Schilling got the jump on the Yankees.

MUSCLING UP: With Barry Bonds on hand with commissioner Bud Selig, Arizona's Craig Counsell imitated the new season homer king by going deep against Mike Mussina (above). After Yankees right fielder David Justice failed in his bid to make a leaping catch of the smash, Counsell received the glad hand when he reached the Diamondbacks' dugout.

COUNSELL
4

WE ♥ NY
BUT NOT THE YANKEES
GO DIAMONDBACKS

TO ERR IS HUMAN: When a fly ball glanced off his glove for an error, David Justice heard from the boo-birds. On the other hand, the Phoenix faithful appreciated Arizona center fielder Steve Finley's effort (immediate right) on a looping double by Scott Brosius and Diamondbacks second baseman Craig Counsell's ability to flag down a ball.

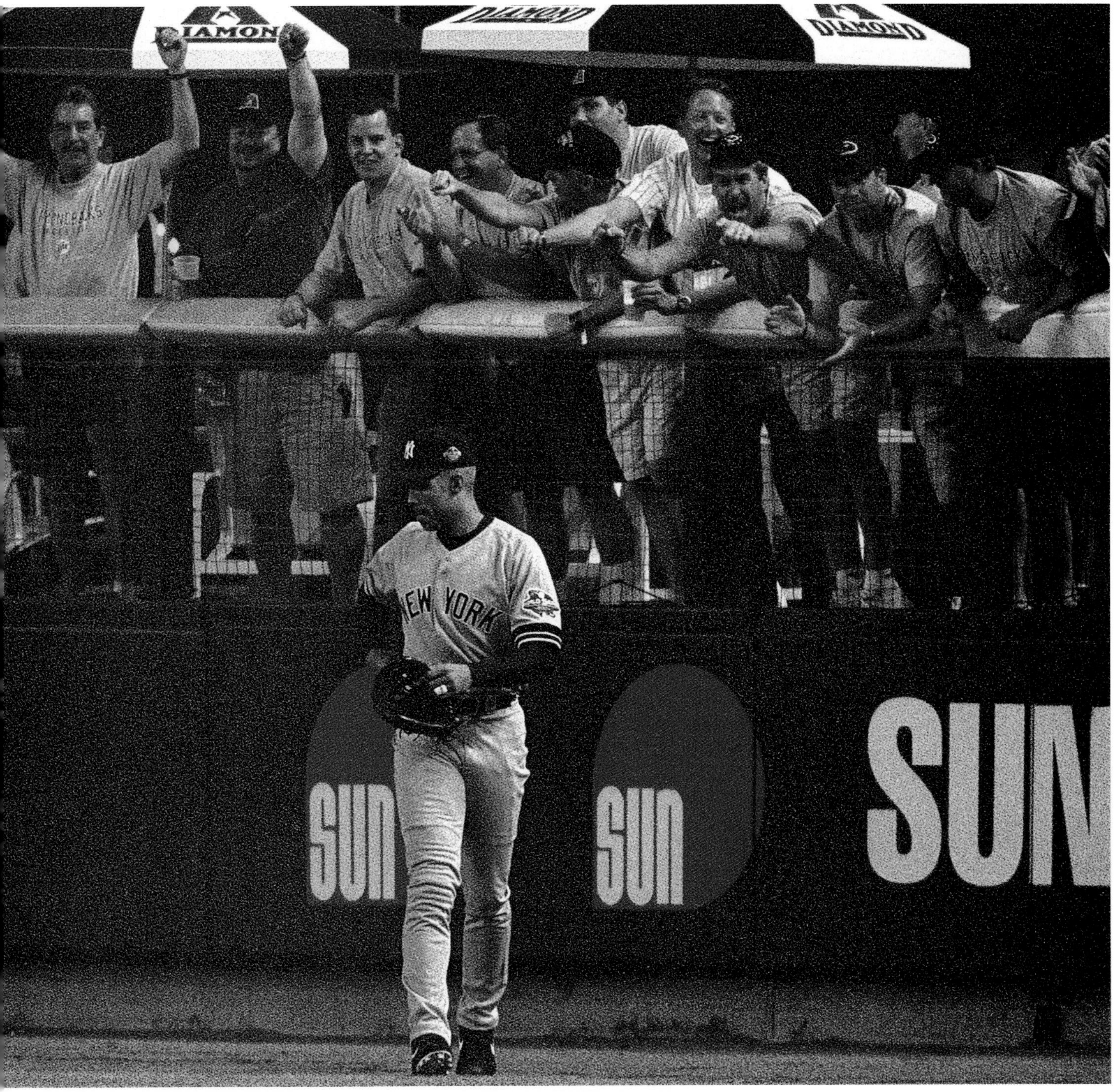
DIAMOND
DIAMOND
DIAMOND
NEW YORK
SUN
SUN
SUN

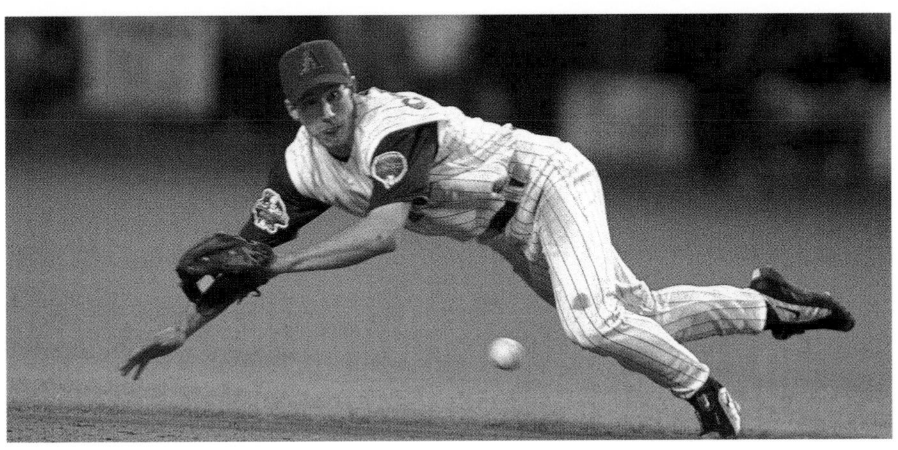

DEPENDS ON YOUR VANTAGE POINT: The view was good from the Diamondbacks' dugout, where Curt Schilling (with towel) watched Luis Gonzalez (left) belt a home run and his relief corps wrap up a one-sided victory, after which Schilling led the applause. The view wasn't so good from the Yankees' dugout, where Scott Brosius (top), perhaps contemplating an error he had made, saw New York come up woefully short in Game 1.

2001 WORLD SERIES, GAME 2

Diamondbacks 4 Yankees 0

It's a real classic for first-timer Johnson

A veteran of 14 major league seasons, lefthander Randy Johnson had never appeared in a World Series until Game 2 of the 2001 Fall Classic.

Johnson, 38, made up for lost time.

A three-time Cy Young Award winner, Johnson went out and shut down the Yankees on a measly three singles—and struck out 11 batters along the way.

The victory boosted Arizona to a two-games-to-none lead over the Yankees, who were gunning for their fourth consecutive World Series crown. "But, Johnson cautioned, "this is far from over."

Game 2 itself was far from over until Matt Williams cracked a three-run homer off Andy Pettitte in the seventh inning. And it wasn't over even then—Johnson had to extricate himself from a two-on, no-out jam in the eighth inning, but he did just that by getting a strikeout and inducing a double-play grounder.

Now it was on to Yankee Stadium, where the Diamondbacks would be put to the test in an atmosphere of championship tradition and crowd frenzy.

SAY WHAT? Third baseman Scott Brosius had a few words for the home-plate umpire when, with two runners on base in the eighth inning, he was called out on strikes. Brosius and the Yankees were no match for Randy Johnson, who was an eyeful and then some on the mound.

World Series
2001
Arizona
Backs

A CRUSHER: Matt Williams' three-run homer in the seventh inning sent a big charge through the Phoenix crowd but was a real jolt to New York lefthander Andy Pettitte, who had pitched four-hit, one-run ball to that point.

HAPPINESS IS ... : An ecstatic Randy Johnson outdueled Andy Pettitte and earned an ovation from the crowd. Pettitte threw strikes all night—only 16 of his 80 pitches were balls—but he did plunk Luis Gonzalez (top, far right). Among the few things the Yankees could cheer was nailing Danny Bautista at the plate. One thing everyone could cheer was Ray Charles' "America the Beautiful."

2001 WORLD SERIES, GAME 3

Yankees 2 Diamondbacks 1

Clemens comes up big for the Yankees

As sensational as he has been since first stepping on a major league pitching mound in 1984, Roger Clemens hasn't been quite as overwhelming in postseason play. So, when he was given the ball for Game 3, he absolutely, positively had to deliver big time. After all, Clemens' Yankees could scarcely afford to go down three games to none in the 2001 World Series.

Clemens, taking a cue from President George W. Bush's ceremonial first-pitch strike, absolutely, positively delivered big time. The fired-up righthander struck out nine Arizona batters in seven innings, permitting only three hits and one run, and put the Yankees back into Series contention with his clutch performance.

Still, the game was tight, and New York needed a typical lights-out effort from closer Mariano Rivera to wrap up matters. Rivera didn't disappoint, retiring all six Diamondbacks batters he faced.

Lefthander Brian Anderson, who struggled in the regular season (4-9 record, 5.20 ERA), pitched creditably for the Diamondbacks. But the Yankees nicked him for a run in the second (a homer by Jorge Posada) and scored another in the sixth—and that's all the Clemens/Rivera tandem needed.

"After this game, I don't think he'll have to defend himself again (from criticism over his postseason pitching)," Yankees manager Joe Torre said of Clemens. "He was dynamite."

AMERICA AND BASEBALL: It was an emotional scene when the World Series moved to New York, where, seven weeks earlier, terrorist attacks had taken a heavy toll of American lives. Chants of "U-S-A! U-S-A! U-S-A!" rang out at Yankee Stadium during a night that featured an appearance by President George W. Bush, the flying of a tattered flag from the site of the collapsed World Trade Center, the waving of countless other flags throughout the storied park and a flight by the eagle Challenger. And, in traditional pregame ceremonies, managers of the rival teams—Bob Brenly of the National League champion Diamondbacks and Joe Torre of the American League champion Yankees—exchanged greetings and their players were introduced.

ADVANTAGE, YANKEES: The Roger Clemens-vs.-Brian Anderson matchup in Game 3 appeared to be a mismatch. Clemens, coming off a 20-3 year, had won 280 games in his career; Anderson, relegated to the bullpen toward the end of the 2001 regular season, had 55 lifetime victories. But it was a 1-1 game heading into the sixth inning.

CATCH AS CATCH CAN: Catcher Damian Miller was somewhere in the vicinity when the Diamondbacks misplayed three catchable popups in Game 3 (first baseman Mark Grace banged into him on one of the Arizona blunders). Also, shortstop Tony Womack booted a grounder (below) as the D-backs had a difficult time latching onto the ball. Arizona pitchers uncorked three wild pitches as well on a night when the N.L. champs exhibited little textbook baseball and created considerable chaos on the basepaths.

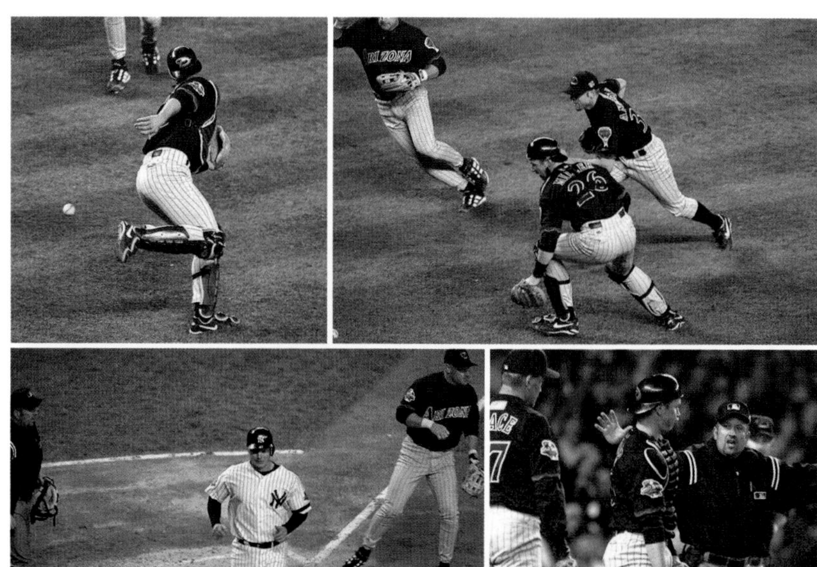

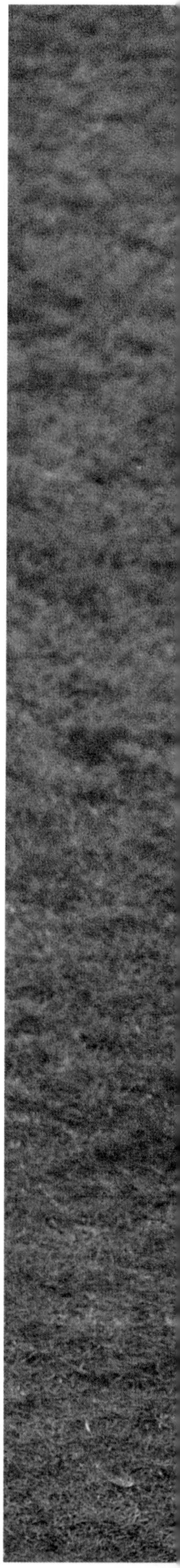

GRACE
17

TWO ON THE SCOREBOARD: New York got the runs it needed in Game 3 when Jorge Posada (above) homered in the second inning and Scott Brosius cracked an RBI single in the sixth off a disgusted Mike Morgan (inset, opposite page), who had relieved the Diamondbacks' Brian Anderson earlier in the inning. Posada eased into a trot after running past Yankees first-base coach Lee Mazzilli.

A BUSY NIGHT AT THE STADIUM: Although the teams combined for only three runs, there was action aplenty in Game 3 of the World Series. In the eighth inning, Yankees closer Mariano Rivera scrambled to tag out Craig Counsell after fielding his bunt (above sequence). Earlier (left to right), Arizona center fielder Steve Finley hauled in Tino Martinez's long smash, the Yankees' Derek Jeter surveyed the situation after being forced at second base on a double play and New York's Paul O'Neill slid into second with a stole base.

2001 WORLD SERIES, GAME 4

Yankees 4 Diamondbacks 3

Miracle in the Bronx, the stunning first act

The Yankees were batting in the bottom of the ninth inning at Yankee Stadium, down by two runs. There were two men out and one runner on base. Byung-Hyun Kim was pitching for Arizona.

Tino Martinez then stepped to the plate and hammered the ball over the fence. Tie game. An inning later, with the clock slipping just past midnight, Derek Jeter became Mr. November by hitting a two-out homer to right field off Kim. The Yankees, one out away from trailing three games to one, had now evened matters in the 97th World Series.

CALENDAR BOY: Derek Jeter supplied some Yankees magic just after October passed into history, blasting a homer off Byung-Hyun Kim in the 10th inning after the reliever had retired the first two New York batters in the inning.

"Surprising things happen," Yankees manager Joe Torre said. "Yet, when you think about it, it doesn't surprise you because this ballclub never quits."

The Diamondbacks' Curt Schilling never quits, either. Asking for and getting the ball—this was the first time he had ever pitched in the majors on only three days' rest—Schilling was merely outstanding.

Answering critics who questioned whether he could come back so quickly, Schilling allowed one run and three hits over seven innings and struck out nine. But after Arizona broke a 1-1 tie with two runs in the eighth, D-backs manager Bob Brenly decided to turn things over to Kim—with disastrous results.

With one out in the Yankees' ninth, Paul O'Neill singled. Kim then struck out the dangerous Bernie Williams, but Martinez swung at the first pitch he saw and drilled a homer to right-center to jolt the D-backs and re-energize the Yankees and their fans. After Kim retired the first two batters in the 10th, Jeter sent the Yankee Stadium throng into ecstasy with his blast.

"We had a lead, we had six outs left to go," said Brenly, who first was taken to task for using Schilling with so little rest and then criticized for taking him out of this game after only 88 pitches. "That's the way we hoped it would work out (Kim getting those six outs). Unfortunately, it didn't."

And suddenly, and remarkably, the World Series was tied.

MR. NOVEMBER

A GAMER: Pitching on three days' rest, Curt Schilling wiped his brow and carried on—and was highly effective in his matchup with Orlando "El Duque" Hernandez (above). The game featured early home runs (opposite page, top) by the Yankees' Shane Spencer and Arizona's Mark Grace and a double play on which the D-backs' Tony Womack was thrown out at the plate.

408
CUMMINGS
13

OUT OF REACH: In the eighth inning, Yankees center fielder Bernie Williams couldn't catch up with Erubiel Durazo's long drive, which went for a double and broke a 1-1 tie. Arizona's lead grew to 3-1 when pinch runner Midre Cummings scored on a grounder.

NEVER-SAY-DIE: When Tino Martinez rescued the Yankees with a game-tying, two-run homer with two out in the ninth inning of Game 4, it seemed too good to be true for the Yankees and too shocking to be real for the Diamondbacks, who commiserated with pitcher Byung-Hyun Kim.

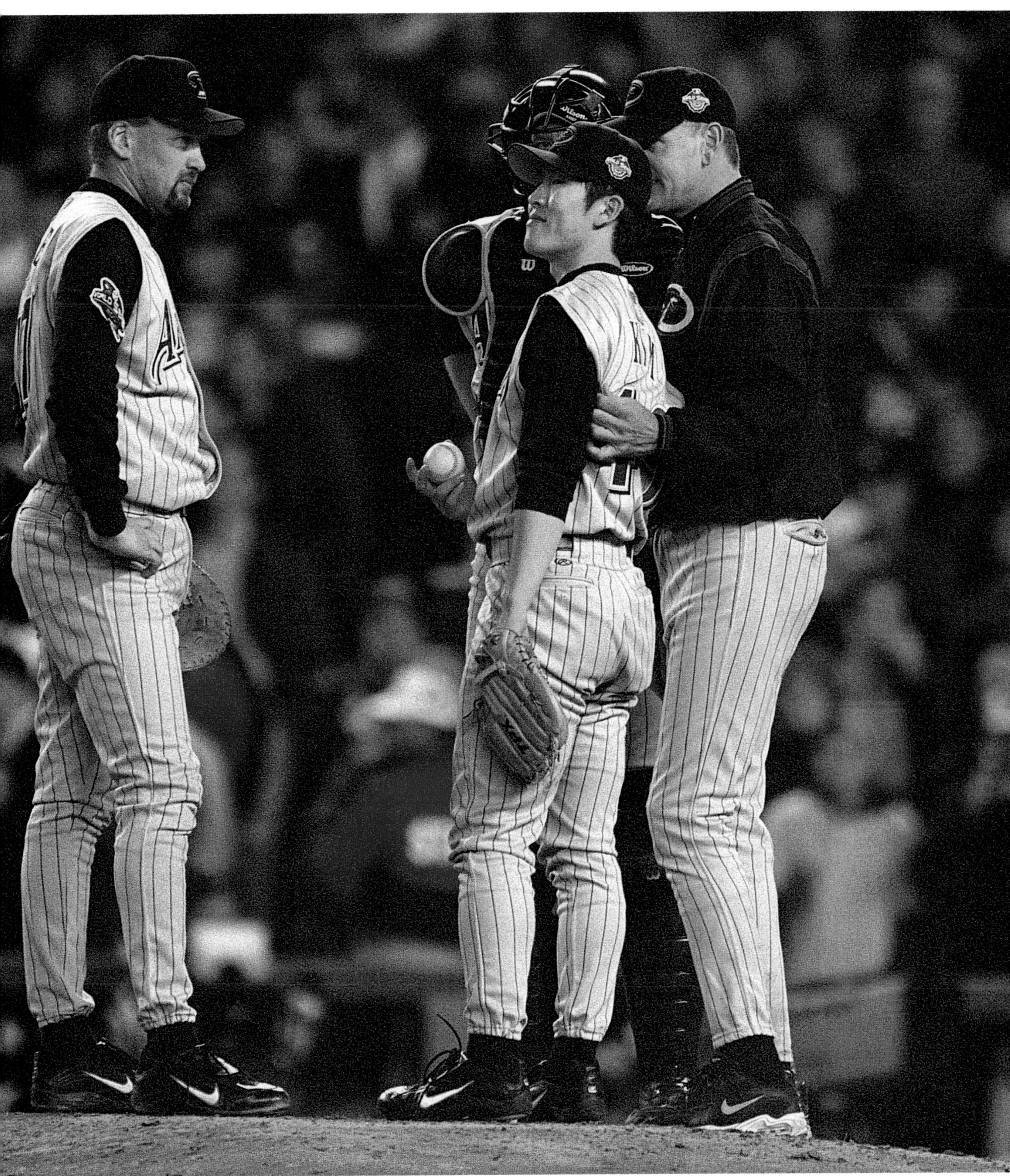

2001 WORLD SERIES, GAME 5

Yankees 3 Diamondbacks 2

Bronx miracle, the second act

The Yankees were batting in the bottom of the ninth inning at Yankee Stadium, down by two runs. There were two men out and one runner on base. Byung-Hyun Kim was pitching for Arizona.

Scott Brosius then stepped to the plate and hammered the ball over the fence. Tie game.

Hadn't we seen all this just the night before?

Incredible. Surreal. Impossible. You pick the word. Maybe, just maybe, it was two words: *Yankee mystique.*

Then, three innings later, Alfonso Soriano singled in the game-winning run. The Yankees, who had been one out away from falling behind three games to two in the World Series (with Arizona's Randy Johnson and Curt Schilling ready to pitch again in Phoenix), now led by that count.

Kim, who had thrown 61 pitches the evening before, inexplicably was called upon again in Game 5 on a night in which starter Miguel Batista gave the Diamondbacks 7⅔ innings of stellar work (no runs, five hits). With Arizona ahead, 2-0, Kim entered the game at the start of the Yanks' ninth and allowed a leadoff double to Jorge Posada. Shane Spencer grounded out and Chuck Knoblauch struck out, but, in an absolutely unbelievable moment in view of what had transpired 24 hours earlier, Brosius homered to left.

Fast forward to the Yankees' 12th: With Albie Lopez pitching for the Diamondbacks, Knoblauch singled and moved to second on Brosius' sacrifice. Soriano followed with a single to right and, again, there was bedlam.

JUMPING FOR JOY: Chuck Knoblauch was airborne after scoring the winning run in another improbable Yankees victory, this one wrapping up on Alfonso Soriano's single in the 12th inning.

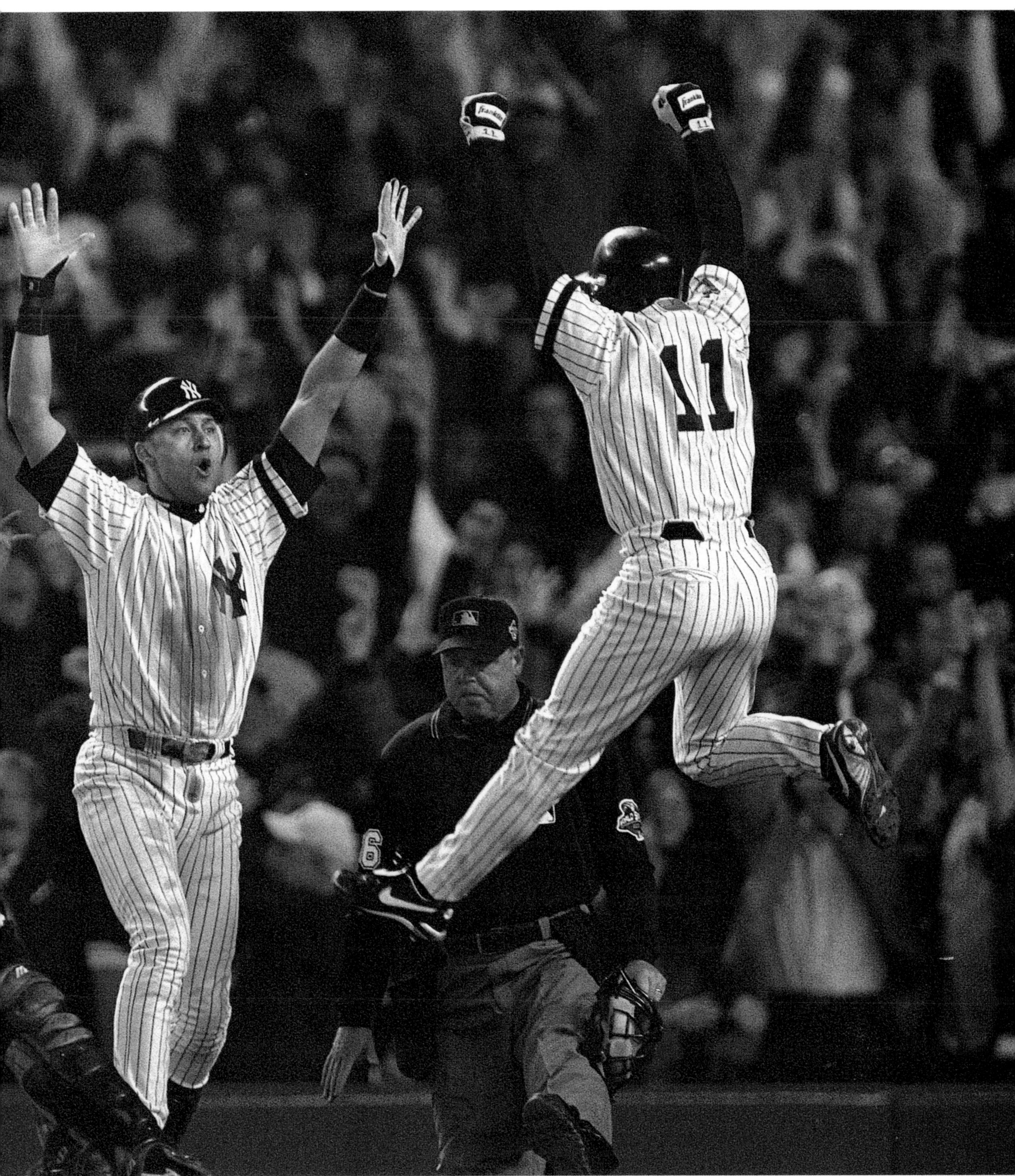
11

IT'S NEVER OVER UNTIL ... : A sign near the World Series bunting probably said it best after the Yankees rallied again in Game 5. Chuck Knoblauch (far left) started the Yankees' 12th with a single, moved to second on Scott Brosius' sacrifice and scored (bottom sequence) on a single by Alfonso Soriano (left, middle), who got congratulations at first base. The triumph, which gave New York the World Series lead over Arizona for the first time, was the Yankees' 10th straight in Series games played at Yankee Stadium.

A CONTACT SPORT: Bases-empty home runs in the fifth inning by Rod Barajas (top) and Steve Finley (above) gave Arizona a 2-0 lead in a fierce pitching duel between the Diamondbacks' Miguel Batista and New York's Mike Mussina (both opposite page). Besides home run trots in Game 5, there was action on the bases, too—with the Yankees' Derek Jeter being nailed by Arizona second baseman Craig Counsell on a double play and the Diamondbacks' Tony Womack getting tangled up with shortstop Jeter when Womack stole a base.

DEJA VU: Scott Brosius' game-tying homer with two out in the ninth inning thrilled the Yankees and their fans but devastated Arizona reliever Byung-Hyun Kim, who had endured all this just the night before. After glimpsing Brosius as the Yankee toured the bases, the disconsolate Kim was taken out of the game by manager Bob Brenly.

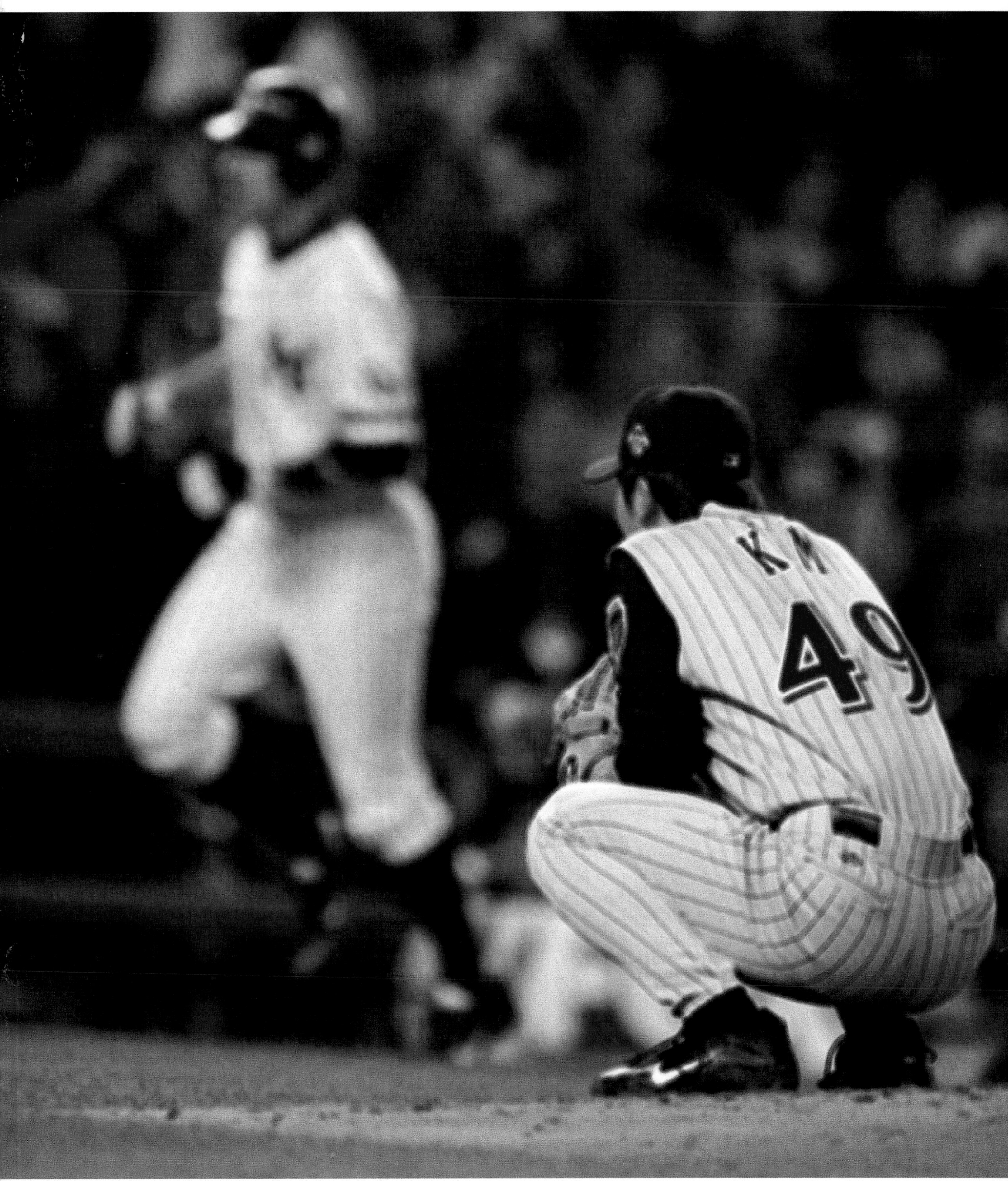

2001 WORLD SERIES, GAME 6

Diamondbacks 15 Yankees 2

ARIZONA DIAMONDBAC
THE DIAMONDBACKS HAVE
BROKE THE ALL TIME RECO
FOR HITS IN ONE WORLD
SERIES GAME WITH 21
BALL 0 STRIKE 0

Diamondbacks stick it to Yankees

After crushing losses at Yankee Stadium in Games 4 and 5 (plus a setback there in Game 3), the Diamondbacks found it uplifting to be back at Bank One Ballpark.

They also found it to be a tonic.

Going from the agony of defeat in New York to the ecstasy of victory in Phoenix, the D-backs came out with a vengeance and clubbed the Yankees with a 22-hit barrage (a World Series record). Arizona led 4-0 after two innings, 12-0 after three, 15-0 after four.

"As heartbreaking as those games were, all three losses in New York, they had no bearing on this game," insisted Arizona manager Bob Brenly after his team forced a seventh game.

Well, maybe. Yet the D-backs appeared possessed. They pasted Yankees starter Andy Pettitte for six runs and seven hits in two innings-plus and were unmerciful against reliever Jay Witasick. Danny Bautista contributed three hits and five RBIs for Arizona; Reggie Sanders had four hits; Matt Williams had two doubles in one inning, Arizona's eight-run third; and Tony Womack banged out three hits. Even pitcher Randy Johnson had a hit, an RBI and two runs scored.

Johnson worked seven innings, yielding only six hits and two runs. Having absorbed his seventh consecutive postseason loss in the N.L. Division Series, he now had won four straight postseason decisions—two in the NLCS and two in the World Series. And with this Fall Classic moving to a Game 7, Johnson didn't rule out an appearance in the finale. "If I can help in any way," he said, "I'll be available."

BREAKING LOOSE: As Damian Miller scored a second-inning run for Arizona, Yankees pitcher Andy Pettitte tried to maintain his focus. Arizona's Randy Johnson (top), who pitched standout ball once again, scored later in the inning and also crossed the plate in the third, leaving Diamondbacks fans with their own candidate for postseason acclaim.

THE HIT MEN: Arizona's eight-run third inning in Game 6 was spiced by nine hits, which, in order, came from (opposite page, left to right, starting at top) Matt Williams, Reggie Sanders, Jay Bell, Damian Miller, Randy Johnson, Danny Bautista, Luis Gonzalez, Greg Colbrunn and Williams (again). Andy Pettitte was pulled from the game early in the inning, then pondered his performance in the dugout.

PANORAMA: It wasn't a pretty scene for the Yankees as they batted in the sixth inning of Game 6. Arizona, with Randy Johnson throwing heat, already had 19 hits and led, 15-0.

AT BAT
INDIVIDUAL BATTING
AVG. GAMES AB
17 200 6 15
jiffy lube®
PENNZOIL
QUAKER STATE
NEW YORK

A ROUT: Manager Joe Torre (below), watching his team take a beating, and reliever Jay Witasick (right) suffered through a long night. Witasick was torched for eight earned runs and 10 hits in $1\frac{1}{3}$ innings. Not everything went right for Arizona—Danny Bautista was thrown out at home plate in the third inning (bottom)—but most things did, resulting in numerous dugout celebrations and postgame congratulations.

YORK

2001 WORLD SERIES, GAME 7

Diamondbacks 3 Yankees 2

Final twist: D-backs pull it out

As closer extraordinaire Mariano Rivera walked to the mound to pitch the ninth inning of Game 7 of the 2001 World Series, the New York Yankees were three outs away from winning their fourth consecutive World Series crown. You could picture a familiar scene: the Yankees soon running out onto the field, fists raised in jubilation. Yet another championship.

CHAMPS: Randy Johnson and Curt Schilling shared the MVP award in the World Series, which ended on a hit by Luis Gonzalez (opposite page). Gonzalez, a 12-year veteran playing in his first Series, appeared happy enough to cry.

Diamondbacks players and fans dreamed otherwise despite the Yankees' 2-1 lead. And, yes, dreams do come true. Even against the mighty Yankees.

Mark Grace, who had never sniffed the World Series in 13 years as a Chicago Cub, led off with a single. Rivera then made a bad throw to second on Damian Miller's bunt, and Arizona had runners on first and second with no one out. Still, that man Rivera was out there, and he was capable of resolving matters in a hurry. Pinch hitter Jay Bell was up next, and he bunted into a force play at third. Tony Womack followed with a game-tying double down the right-field line, and the Phoenix crowd erupted.

Rivera proceeded to hit Craig Counsell with a pitch, loading the bases. With the infield drawn in, Luis Gonzalez looped a single into left-center. As stunning and as unfathomable as those fantastic Yankee finishes in New York, Game 7 and the World Series itself were over. And, in the climactic twist of this Fall Classic, it was the Diamondbacks who were running out onto the field, fists raised.

Arizona, which outscored the Yankees 37-14 in the seven games, was the World Series champion in only its fourth season as a major league franchise. Previously, Florida had made the fastest trip to the top by an expansion team (five years).

Curt Schilling, again pitching on only three days' rest, and Roger Clemens had been locked in a tense 0-0 tie until the sixth, when the D-backs broke through on Danny Bautista's RBI double. But the Yankees countered with a run in the seventh, and they seized the lead when Alfonso Soriano homered off Schilling in the eighth. With the specter of Rivera trudging out of the bullpen in the bottom half of the eighth, a Yankees victory appeared inevitable.

Not this time.

The winning pitcher in this classic Game 7? None other than Randy Johnson, who hurled the final 1⅓ innings for the Diamondbacks and racked up a record-equaling third victory in one World Series.

25

DUELING PITCHERS: Curt Schilling (above) and Roger Clemens were in a scoreless duel until the sixth, when Arizona's Steve Finley (congratulated by Mark Grace) scored on Danny Bautista's double. The Yankees tied the game in the seventh, then took the lead in the eighth on a homer by Alfonso Soriano (far right). Clemens, who was taken out of the game in the seventh, saw the chance for a first-inning Yankees lead evaporate when Paul O'Neill (opposite page, top) was thrown out while trying to stretch a double into a triple.

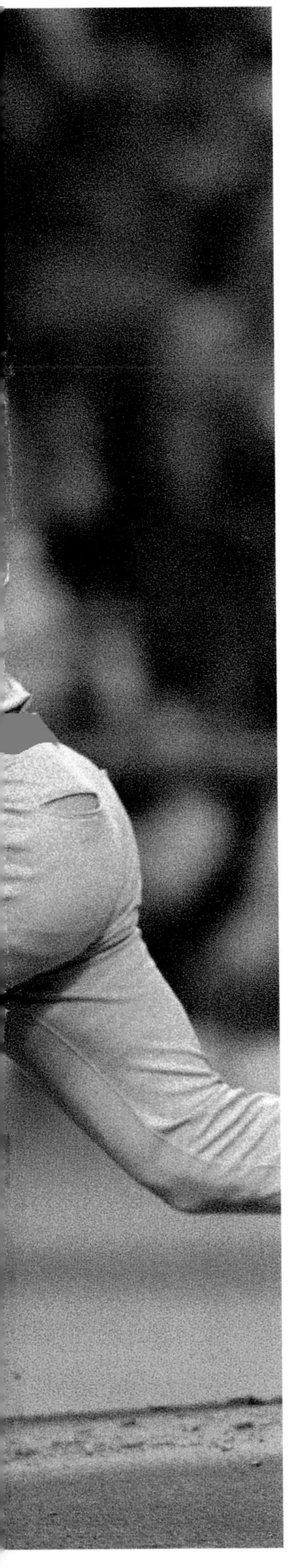

NEW YORK

GRACE
17

NEW

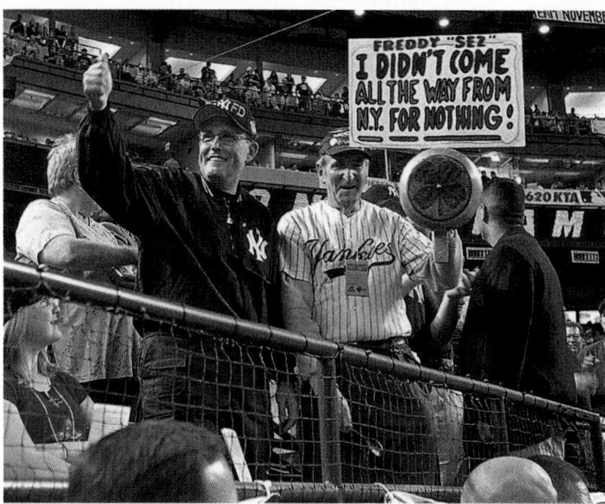

ACTION CENTRAL: Center fielder Steve Finley (top) continued his fine defensive play for Arizona in Game 7, a contest in which Craig Counsell reached base on a botched play at first and Danny Bautista was called out at third (opposite page, top) after doubling home the game's first run. New York mayor Rudy Giuliani and other Yankees fans offered vocal support for their team, which got a rally-igniting hit in the seventh from Derek Jeter (who, immediate left, had struck out in the first inning).

DOWN, BUT NOT OUT: With the usually impenetrable Mariano Rivera (top, left) on the mound for the Yankees, Arizona faced a daunting task as it tried to overcome a 2-1 deficit in the ninth. But a single, an error and a forceout gave the D-backs a chance, and Tony Womack (top, swinging) followed with a game-tying double that scored pinch runner Midre Cummings (above). And, after a hit batsman loaded the bases, Luis Gonzalez (immediate right) lofted a World Series-winning hit over a drawn-in infield. The single drove in Jay Bell (opposite page, top, right), setting off a wild celebration at Bank One Ballpark. The jubilant Gonzalez got a big hug from coach Eddie Rodriguez.

WILLIAMS
9

REYNOSO
27
32